*St. Cecilia seated at her organ
by Carlo Dolci.*

Engraved by J.J. Waddington Ltd

The

Story of Notation

BY

C. F. ABDY WILLIAMS

M.A., Mus. Bac.

GREENWOOD PRESS, PUBLISHERS
NEW YORK

Originally published in 1903
by the Walter Scott Publishing Co.

First Greenwood Reprinting, 1969

Library of Congress Catalogue Card Number 68-57648

SBN 8371-1622-8

PRINTED IN UNITED STATES OF AMERICA

Preface.

THE roots of our modern musical system lie so deeply embedded in antiquity that it is impossible to trace the early history of its notation without reference to the Greek system from which it has sprung; and this involves the use of certain words, found in ancient treatises, which are as unfamiliar to modern musicians and Greek scholars as the technicalities of modern musical structure are to the general public.

Those who may be alarmed at the lengthy and strange-looking words used by Greek musicians are recommended to omit Chapter II.; but at the same time it must not be forgotten that the inconvenience of these long words was the very thing that necessitated the invention of a musical notation by which sounds could be represented on paper, or parchment, or stone, in a small compass.

Story of Notation

My thanks are due to Signor A. Fiordelisi di Manco, of the National Library at Naples; to Cavaliere Pagliara, Librarian of the Conservatorio in the same city; and to the Rev. F. W. Galpin, for the important works they have placed at my disposal.

C. F. ABDY WILLIAMS.

MILFORD-ON-SEA,
May 1903.

Contents

————•••————

CHAPTER I.

CHAPTER II.

vii

Story of Notation

CHAPTER III.

CHAPTER IV.

CHAPTER V.

Contents

CHAPTER VI.

CHAPTER VII.

Story of Notation

CHAPTER VIII.

CHAPTER IX.

CHAPTER X.

Contents

CHAPTER XI.

CHAPTER XII.

ATTEMPTS TO INVENT NEW FORMS OF NOTATION, AND TO REFORM THE OLD.

List of Illustrations.

——•◦•——

List of Illustrations

xiii

Story of Notation

List of Illustrations

Story of Notation

The
Story of Notation.

———◆———

CHAPTER I.

OUTLINE OF THE HISTORY OF THE REPRESENTATION OF MUSICAL SOUNDS IN WRITING.

The Greek notation—Other ancient notations—Tables of Greek notation—Greek time-signs — Boethius—Neumes—Latin alphabetical notation—Beginnings of harmony.

THE representation of musical sounds in writing, called musical notation, or simply notation, from *nota*, a mark or sign, is a thing so commonplace, so universal, and apparently so simple, that we are apt to overlook the fact that our stave, with its variously shaped "notes" and all that goes to convey a composer's thoughts to the world, are the outcome of centuries of experiments and gradual improvements. Whether the Egyptians, the Hebrews, Chaldeans, and other Semitic nations, which had arrived at a certain degree of musical culture, noted their music is not known; it may be presumed

I

Story of Notation

that they did, but up to the present nothing has been discovered of the nature of a musical semeiography.[1]

It cannot be said that these nations were not yet sufficiently advanced to be able to invent a means of writing down the various sounds of voices and instruments: the fact remains that, as far as we know at present, the Greeks were the only ancient European nation that did so, and they made use of letters of the alphabet for this purpose, as did the Hindoos before them, and the Western Europeans after them; the Persians used numbers, and a kind of stave of nine lines, between which the numbers were placed, while the Chinese used special signs for their pentatonic scale.

The Greek Notation

Other Ancient Notations

The history of our present notation begins with that of the Greeks, who arranged their alphabet in groups of three letters to each tone, thus showing the semitones and quarter-tones. The knowledge of this arrangement passed away until rediscovered in the nineteenth century by the labours of Bellermann, Fortlage, and others, who

---

[1] In early stages of musical development it seems that certain traditional melodic patterns or forms, to which names are given, form the foundation of compositions. Such are the *Ragas* of the Southern Indians of to-day, the *Nomes* of ancient Greece, and in all probability the "Tunes" of which the names are preserved in the titles of some of the Psalms, such as Neginoth, Nehiloth, Gittith, etc. As long as the musicians' skill was chiefly exercised in making what we should call "variations" on these traditional forms, a notation would not be a necessity, since it would be easy enough to teach by ear variations of a well-known melody.

Introductory Sketch

have explained the notation tables given by Alypius, Aristides, Nicomachus, Ptolemy, Gaudentius,[1] and later writers. The tables, arranged according to tropes and modes, show successions of **Tables of** letters, apparently taken at haphazard, to **Greek** indicate the seven notes of the three kinds **Notation** of scale, the diatonic, chromatic, and enharmonic.

The Greeks also used a system of time-signs, two of which have survived to the present day in the long (-) and short (ᴗ) signs placed over vowels in Latin grammars, and they had **Greek** means of representing accent, so that their **Time-signs** notation was as complete as the mediæval tablatures, of which we shall speak later, or the modern tonic sol-fa.

The first use of Latin letters for representing musical sounds is found in the writings of Boe- thius, about A.D. 500; though it is a **Boethius** mistake to speak of the "Boethian notation," since he never used the letters to indicate musical melodies.[2]

---

[1] Greek writers on music of the first few centuries of the Christian era. Their treatises are preserved in manuscript in various European libraries, and were printed by Meibomius and Wallis in the seventeenth century, with Latin translations. They have been translated also into French and German, but not as yet into English.

[2] Boethius was a poet and philosopher who flourished about A.D. 500. He was the author of a famous Latin treatise on music, the study of which was greatly pursued all through the Middle Ages, and which was the chief subject for examinations for musical degrees at Oxford and Cambridge until a comparatively recent period.

Story of Notation

After his time there arose a system of signs called neumes, from the Greek νεῦμα, a nod or sign, derived **Neumes** from the Greek accents; and contemporary with this, the Latin letters began to be used to represent the degrees of the scale, though not in any uniform manner until systematised by **Latin** Guido of Arezzo in the eleventh century; **Alphabetical Notation** while by the addition of lines to the neumes nine hundred years ago, our stave was invented. By this time a new form of music had arisen, in which the voices sang different melodies, and it **Beginnings of Harmony** became imperatively necessary to find some system which should absolutely indicate both the exact pitch and the exact time value of the sounds to be sung; and the history of notation from the eleventh century to the sixteenth is a story of the efforts made by churchmen who, hampered by theological difficulties, by morbid scruples over the meanings of words, and a contempt for the more practical efforts of the worldly musicians, painfully evolved something like a satisfactory system, upon which the latter were able eventually to graft their own results; and so the notation, as we know it, was completed.

The history of notation is a story of human effort sustained over many centuries towards the attainment of one object. To follow all its details would require a work of some magnitude and an immense number of facsimiles. Interesting accounts have been written by Hugo Riemann in German, and by David and Lussy

4

Introductory Sketch

in French. In the succeeding chapters we propose to
follow out, with as much detail as space permits, the
story of which we have given an outline, and afterwards,
to give short accounts of some of the hundreds of
attempts which have been made to supersede the system
that has taken so many centuries, and so much painful
effort, to perfect.

CHAPTER II.

" Ancient musicians invented certain little notes by which a melody could be handed down to posterity."—BOETHIUS.

THE Greeks are known to have used from prehistoric times a variety of stringed instruments, plucked like

Ancient Stringed Instruments the harp with the fingers, afterwards with the fingers or a plectrum of bone, wood, or metal, and finally with the fingers of the left hand and a plectrum in the right hand simultaneously. These instruments were of many shapes and sizes, but in principle they were all alike : a number of strings of equal or nearly equal

Ancient Stringed Instruments

length were stretched over a sounding-box by means of a cross bar, supported by two horns, which projected above the sounding-box.

After the introduction of the plectrum, the more ancient method of playing —*i.e.*, with the fingers, was called Psalmos; singing to such playing was called Psalmodia; and an instrument, when thus played, was called Psalterion. Hence our words Psalm, Psalmody, and Psaltery.

It is not to our purpose to give a description of

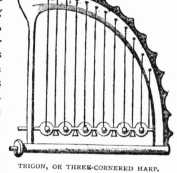

TRIGON, OR THREE-CORNERED HARP.

the many shapes, which the illustrations sufficiently show, of these little instruments: the list of names given by Pollux includes the Lyre, Kithara, or Cithara, Barbiton, Chelys, Psalterion, Trigon, Sambuca, Pectis, Phorminx, Phenix, Spadix, Phœnician Lyre, Clepsiambos, Pariambos, Iambucus, Scindapsus, and the Epigoneion, which had forty strings. **Varieties of Stringed Instruments** Other authors mention the Simikion, which had thirty-five strings; the Magadis, an Egyptian instrument of twenty strings, in which the **Magadis** octave of each string was produced, though whether this was done by dividing the string into the proportion of

7

Story of Notation

2 : 1 by means of the bridge, *Magas,* or merely tuning the instrument an octave above another instrument, as our so-called piccolo is tuned an octave above the flute, is not known. From this instrument comes the verb to "magadise," meaning to sing or play in octaves. The names that chiefly concern us are the Kithara or Lyre of seven strings, the Epigoneion, the Simikion, and the Magadis, since Greek notation seems to have been developed in connection with these instruments.

The principle of stopping a string by the left hand on a finger-board, as in the guitar, violin, etc., though practised by the Egyptians, and known to the Greeks, does not seem to have been favoured by the latter; and it is through instruments of the lyre tribe that we know the names of the various sounds in the Greek scales, and the signs used to represent them in writing. At first the Lyre had four, or even only three **The Lyre** strings, and it is probable, though not capable of proof, that the four-stringed lyre was tuned to what afterwards became the normal, or Dorian tetrachord, represented by a semitone and two tones, as our B, C, D, E, and the three-stringed lyre may have been used for the enharmonic tetrachord B, C, E, before the semitone B, C was divided into quarter-tones. Or the four-stringed lyre may have been tuned to a tetrachordal scale used by some South Sea Islanders at the Paris Exhibition of 1878, C, F, G, C. Tetrachords took such an important place in the Greek musical system that we cannot go far wrong if we assume that

8

The Greek Systems

the earliest instruments were tuned to some kind of tetrachordal scale.

Terpander[1] is said by Cleonides (Pseudo-Euclid) to have increased the number of strings from four to seven, probably by adding a second tetrachord above the first, forming a heptachord system—

**First
Improve-
ment in
the Lyre**

B C D E F G A

The "system" or scale was gradually extended by the addition of tetrachords until it was developed into two "perfect" systems, which give us our keyboard and the names of its keys.

**Perfect
Systems**

The Greater Perfect System consisted of four tetrachords, or two heptachords, and was completed by "Proslambanomenos," "the added sound."

Proslambanomenos | B C D E F G a b c d e f g a
A |

This system was also called *Disjunct,* owing to the fresh start above the middle a, where the two tetrachords are "disjoined." The Lesser Perfect System, called the *Conjunct* System, consisted of three tetrachords, with Proslambanomenos.

**Disjunct
and
Conjunct
Systems**

Prosl. | B C D E F G a b♭ c d
A |

The reader will perceive that a new note, B flat, is here

[1] Flourished B.C. 676.

9

Story of Notation

introduced, in order to bring the conjunct tetrachord into agreement with the others as to its intervals; the tetrachord prevailed over the octave at this time, and allowed a B natural and a B flat to occur in the same scale. This B flat played a very important part in music all through the mediæval times.

We have now got as our working basis the point at which the history of the scales in use at **The Begin-** the present day begins, apart from myths **ning of** and traditions; and with the completion **Musical** of the greater perfect system the history of **Notation** musical notation begins.

The naming and writing down of musical sounds was

FEMALE DANCERS TUNING AND PLAYING LYRES.

naturally used for instruments before being used for voices; and the intervals sung take their names from the strings of the instruments. One can easily observe what

Notation Systems

goes on in childhood : a baby of very tender years will soon learn to sing a tune in imitation of its elders ; but the same baby finds it far more difficult to pick out the same tune on an instrument. "Playing by ear" is a very much more complicated and difficult process than "singing by ear"; and some sort of guide to show what succession of strings to strike soon becomes indispensable.

Gevaert[1] points out that the systems of musical notation known up to the present day may be divided into two classes. The first, which is that of the Chinese, Hindoos, Modern Arabs, the Gregorians, the Ancient Greeks, and the Tonic Sol-faists, he calls "phonetic"—that is to say, the sounds are represented by alphabetical letters, arithmetical figures, or by words. The second class, in which the upward and downward movement of the voice, or sounds of the instrument, is represented more or less pictorially by higher and lower positions of the signs which indicate the sounds, he calls "diastematic," from a Greek word signifying interval. It would not be amiss to call it a pictorial system. To this class belong the liturgical notations of the Jews, Abyssinians, Byzantines, Armenians, the neumes of the ancient Church, and our present system, which, as we shall see later, is a combination of the neumatic and the phonetic notations. It is natural that the

Classification of Notation Systems

Phonetic Notation

Notation by Intervals

---

[1] *Hist. de la Musique de l'Antiquité*, vol. i. p. 394.

11

Story of Notation

The conception of sounds as high and low is arbitrary phonetic should precede the pictorial method: for that the longer or slacker string should produce a "low" sound, and the shorter and tighter string a "high" sound, is entirely an arbitrary conception; and it has been within our experience that persons destitute of musical knowledge have been unable to grasp the idea that the treble sounds of a piano are "higher" than the bass.

The Greeks named the sounds by length of String The conception of high and low as applied to sound seems to have come to the Greeks but slowly; and when they were obliged for teaching purposes to give names to the strings of their lyre, they called the lowest string of the tetrachord *Hypate,* which means "highest," for in instruments of the harp shape, such as the trigon, this string was the "highest" when placed upright, or, as we should say, the longest. Starting from proslambanomenos, the names of the strings were as follows:—

Modern Names.	Greek Name of String.	Explanation.
A	Proslambanomenos	"Added" string.
B	Hypate hypatōn	"Highest" string of the "highest" tetrachord (producing the lowest sound).
C	Parhypate hypatōn	"Next to highest" of "highest" tetrachord.

Strings of the Lyre

Modern Names.	Greek Name of String	Explanation.
D	Lichanos hypatōn	"Forefinger" string of highest tetrachord ; it was plucked with the forefinger.
E	Hypate mesōn	"Highest" string of "middle" tetrachord.
F	Parhypate mesōn	"Next to highest" of "middle" tetrachord.
G	Lichanos mesōn	"Forefinger" string of "middle" tetrachord.
A	Mése	"Middle" string. This is the most important note of the whole Greek system. It was the note that gave the pitch for tuning, and its octave has remained so to this day for stringed instruments. It afterwards became the "Dominant" of the Gregorian Chant.
b♮	Trite synnēmenōn	"Third" string of the "conjunct" tetrachord.
c	Lichanos, or Paranēte synnēmenōn	"Forefinger" or "next to lowest" string of "conjunct" tetrachord.
d	Nēte synnēmenōn	"Lowest" of the "conjunct" tetrachord—*i.e.*, the "shortest" string of the Lesser perfect system.

Story of Notation

Modern Names.	Greek Name of String.	Explanation.
b	Paramesos	"Next to middle" (*i.e.*, in the Greater perfect system).
c	Trite diezeugmenon	"Third" string of the "disjunct" tetrachord.
d	Lichanos diezeugmenon	"Forefinger" string of disjunct tetrachord.
e	Nēte diezeugmenon	"Lowest" string of disjunct tetrachord.
f	Trite hyperbolaion	"Third" string of "extreme" tetrachord.
g	Lichanos hyperbolaion	"Forefinger" string of extreme tetrachord.
aa	Nēte hyperbolaion	"Lowest" string of extreme tetrachord. (To us, the *highest* note of the Greek system.)

It is evident from the above list of names that the early Greek musicians had no idea that a sound could be higher or lower than another. Hence it was impossible that they should invent a pictorial notation.

Several of the strings had also other names, with which it is not necessary to trouble the reader. The nomenclature was very unwieldy: it is as if we were

14

Alphabetical Notation

to always use the words "Tonic," "Dominant," "Subdominant," "Leading note," etc., in teaching music instead of A, B, C, or the French method *Ut, re, mi.* At a very early period Greek musicians found it necessary to invent a less clumsy method of indicating sounds, and some one suggested the use of the alphabet. It was not the Greek alphabet as we know it, but an early Dorian alphabet, showing traces of Phœnician or Semitic origin. *The unwieldiness of the note names necessitated a form of Notation*

The alphabet having been suggested as a means of representing musical sounds in writing, we moderns would imagine that nothing was simpler than to begin at the top of the scale, or at the bottom, and merely give letters to the strings in alphabetical order. But the inventors did not do this: by some process of reasoning which has not yet been explained, they applied the first letter of the Phœnician-Greek alphabet to the string called *Nēte hyperbolaion* (our aa), and then carried on the alphabet by a remarkable series of octaves, suggesting a probable connection between notation and the magadis, Fig. 1 (*a*). If momentarily leap over some twenty-five centuries we shall find a German alphabetical notation with an almost equally incomprehensible series of *fourths,* of which, however, the explanation is extant (page 156). *Curious arrangement of the Alphabet*

It will be seen that the theoretical scale of two octaves is already extended by the addition of a note below Proslambanomenos; and we shall see later that to suit

Story of Notation

the several modes and transposition keys the complete notation gives a compass of rather over three octaves, which is the limit especially mentioned by Aristoxenus,[1] as possible for voices and instruments. The Epigoneion and Simikion could therefore embrace nearly the whole range of the notation.

FIG. I (a). (*Continued on p.* 24.)

Aleph. Beth. Ghimel. Daleth. He. Vau. - Zain. Cheth.Teth. Iod. Kaph.. Larred (Another
Alpha. Beta Gamma. Delta. Epsilon. Digamma. Zeta. Eta. Theta. Iota. Kappa. Lambda. this same)
(Part of)
form of

The succession of sounds A to aa, together with trite synnemenon (B flat), became known as the Locrian, or Æolian, or Hypodorian, or Common Trope; and, though the point is still much debated, there seems little doubt that its intervals were used in a kind of harmony, so elementary as to seem to us childish; but it must not be forgotten that we are speaking of the earliest infancy of a system of music which in its riper years has produced

The Common Trope

---

[1] Aristoxenus, who flourished about B.C. 300, was a philosopher and musician, and the author of the earliest existing work on music, which seems to consist of a series of lectures given by him to students at Athens. He was a pupil of Aristotle, and the author of no less than five hundred books on various subjects, of which only fragments of two or three are extant; but we are able to gather much of his musical doctrine from allusions to it by other writers.

16

Lyre Accompaniments

the symphonies of a Beethoven and the music dramas of a Wagner. At any rate this early diatonic style, called by Plutarch the style of Olympus and Terpander, was competent to produce simple chords of two sounds; and though the ancient writers **Simultaneous sounds** inform us that the singing together of boys **between** and men, or of women and men, was always **Voice and** done in octaves only, and in no other **Instrument** interval, yet it seems, from a passage in Plato's *Republic,* and from certain passages in Plutarch's short work on Music, that when the lyre accompanied the voice, it frequently sounded a note that was not in unison or octave with the voice.[1]

---

[1] Thus, Plato objects to boys being taught to accompany on the lyre with a melody different from that of the voice, as is done by professional players. An anonymous Greek writer, to whom we shall refer later, speaks of the Crousis or accompaniment. Plutarch says: ".The Ancients (*i.e.,* the musicians of the period of Olympus and Terpander, about B.C. 670) would not have applied the Trite as an accompaniment to Parhypate, if they had not understood its use.

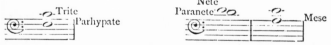

"The note Nete they used in the accompaniment as a diaphony (discord) with Paranete (*i.e.,* lichanos diezeugmenon), and as a symphony (concord) with Mese.

"And not only did they apply the sounds Trite and Paranete thus, but also Nete synnēmenōn, for in the accompaniment they used Nete synnēmenōn as a diaphony (discord) with Paranete, and Parhypate, and as a symphony with Mese and Lichanos." If these words seem strange to the modern reader, let him imagine a teacher of harmony explaining

Story of Notation

We must give a few more details of the Greek musical system, in order to show the reader what their **Movable Sounds** notation was required to express, where it differed from, and where it was similar to ours; and it may help him to an understanding of the so-called "movable sounds" of the Greek tetrachord, if we say that we moderns make use

the matter thus: "The ancients used the Tonic to accompany the Subdominant, the Mediant to accompany the Supertonic and Submediant, the Supertonic to accompany the Tonic, Subdominant, Submediant, and Dominant." In a case of this kind names are more convenient than notation. (See R. Westphal, *Mus. des Griec. Alterthumes*, 1883, p. 62; do., translation of Plutarch's *Music*, p. 46.)

Nete Synnemenon

Paranete Syn.   Parhyp.   Mese   Lichanos

Symphonies or concords were unisons, fourths, fifths, and octaves: all other intervals were diaphonies or discords. We learn from Aristotle's Problem No. 19 that the accompaniment was always above the melody.

Aristotle speaks of this elementary harmony as "Mixis," our word mixing or mingling, and he says that the Mixis had no effect on the character of the music, for character is produced by melody alone (Gevaert, *La Mus. de l'Ant.*, i. p. 336). And here we have the very root of the difference between ancient and modern music, and the reason of the necessity of a difference in the class of notation used. To the Greek the melody alone was all in all: to us a melody suggests a harmonic combination. From our earliest years we are so accustomed to a harmonic accompaniment that a mere "tune" by itself rarely pleases; we imperatively demand harmony, or if we do not get it, we imagine it. The Ancients soon began to require further means of

Fixed Sounds

of "movable sounds" in our scale, for the third may be major or minor, and is "moved" by Beethoven in passages such as those in Sonata op. 31, No. 1, where he alters the mode in alternate pairs of bars: moreover, two "movable" sounds occur in the minor scale, the sixth and seventh being raised in ascending and lowered in descending.

In Greek music the highest and lowest sounds of each tetrachord were tuned to the interval of a perfect

expression than the plain diatonic succession of tones and semitones; and, not having arrived at the conception of singing two or more melodies together, they began to alter the tuning of their instruments in order to produce variety of expression, or, as they would say, to give character to the music; and unfortunately they discovered at about the same time that strings or pipes, divided according to certain mathematical proportions, produced certain definite musical intervals. Thus a string divided by a bridge or the finger in the ratio of 2 : 1 produces the octave of the sound given by the whole string:

The ratio 3 : 2 produces a fifth.
,, 4 : 3 ,, a fourth.
,, 9 : 8 ,, a major tone.
,, 10 : 9 ,, a minor tone.

And so on, till we arrive at mathematical minutiæ that are utterly useless and incomprehensible to the practical musician. Henceforward Greek musicians were divided into two schools: the followers of Pythagoras, who occupied themselves with the mathematics, to the exclusion of the art of music, and the followers of Aristoxenus, a pupil of Aristotle, who referred everything connected with the scale sounds to the ear, and who represented the artistic side of music. Aristides Quintilianus attributes a form of notation to Pythagoras differing from that described by other Greek writers; and as no other writer refers to it, we need do no more than mention it to show that in those days other notations existed besides the one in general use, just as they do now.

Story of Notation

fourth, and were always referred to as the "Fixed Sounds." Proslambanomenos was also a fixed sound,

Fixed Sounds

being tuned an octave below Mese. But the two interior sounds of each tetrachord became at various times, and by various musicians, subjected to an immense variety of alterations; and hence were known as the "Movable Sounds." Any musician practically taught what he liked about the movable sounds.

Now, our own experience that equal temperament,[1] in which every interval except the octave is slightly

Variations in the tuning of intervals would not offend ears untrained to harmony

out of tune, produces no discomfort to us, ought to be sufficient to show us that to a nation which had no conception of harmonic combinations, an alteration of the tuning of the melodic intervals would not appear a very arbitrary proceeding, but would, and actually did, produce a pleasant sensation. To this day the Southern Indian musician alters the pitch of notes by pressing the string behind a high fret; and the singers of South Italy use so strong a vibrato that it is

---

[1] Equal temperament is the term applied to the modern system of tuning organs and pianofortes, by which all the semitones are made equal, and all intervals except the octave are out of tune, but so slightly as to cause no inconvenience to the ear. Up to the middle of the eighteenth century keyed instruments were generally tuned in "unequal" temperament, by which certain keys were perfectly in tune, while others were unbearably harsh. The modern system, which places every key at the disposal of the composer, is an inevitable result of the development of the art of music.

Movable Sounds

really impossible at times to know whether an interval of a small semitone, or a repetition of the same note is intended ; and the audience, accustomed to it, is delighted, and applauds an effect that, to the more stolid northern ear, sounds disagreeable and out of tune.

ROMAN LYRES AND A KITHARA.

The first effort in the direction of altering the tuning of the movable sounds seems to have been made or recorded by Polymnastus, whom Westphal mentions as having possibly been the inventor of the notation.[1] The diatonic scale which is obtained by tuning pure fourths and fifths by ear, as on the modern harp, for example, was altered to the " soft " diatonic of Polymnastus ; in this scale the lichanos of each tetrachord was flattened by a quarter of a tone : producing the intervals (ascending) semitone, $\frac{3}{4}$ tone, $1\frac{1}{4}$ tone.

Soft Diatonic of Polymnastus

---

[1] Westphal, *Mus. des Gr. Alterthumes*, pp. 134, etc.

Story of Notation

The next alteration was the "Middle soft diatonic" used by Archytas. In this, both the movable sounds

Middle Soft Diatonic of Archytas are flattened. And it was to this form of diatonic tetrachord that the notation was applied, for in the diatonic notation the second sound of the tetrachord is invariably shown by a letter representing an interval of less than a semitone above the first. (Comp. Ex., p. 39, with Fig. 2, p. 34.)

We now come to an alteration of the tuning which has puzzled many learned men; yet there is no reason

Quarter Tones why it should. It has been said that no ear could ever have tolerated the intervals of a quarter of a tone which occurred in the

The ear can be trained to appreciate the En- harmonic Genus enharmonic genus; and that they could only have been theoretical and not practical. Yet we not only have constant reference to this genus, but if we tune an instrument to it, we find that our ear soon gets accustomed to it, and, as long as we use no harmony, we soon begin to like these strange minute intervals.

From Plutarch it would appear that the enharmonic genus was invented after the time of Olympus, and

The earliest En- harmonic Tetrachord that it at first consisted in omitting the lichanos, thus producing the intervals semi- tone and major third E͡FA, A͡b♭D, b͡ce, etc. In this case the tetrachord only contained three sounds. But the semitone soon be- came divided into two quarter-tones called *dieses,* and the tetrachord became diesis, diesis, major third, or E F♭ F A. And although the Pythagoreans tried to

22

Enharmonic Dieses

complicate the scale by impossible mathematical distinctions, practical musicians held to the quarter-tones, which they could easily obtain by ear. The Enharmonic is called by Aristoxenus the most beautiful of the genera; and he complains that his contemporaries have, for the most part, lost the art of performing its intervals, whereas their forerunners applied themselves more to this than to any other genus. With the new genus an addition was necessary to the scheme of notation; and it was very simply made, though not in the way we should expect. The new effects were produced by flattening the movable sounds; and we should expect, therefore, that some new sign, corresponding to our flat, would be introduced: but the Greeks had no sign showing a flattening; their notation could only show a sharpening of the sound.

To indicate the two dieses the inventor of the notation simply laid the letter on its back for the first, and reversed it for the second, thus:

Ε Ш Ⴈ, Ϝ ᴚ ⅂, Κ ⋊ ⋉, ⊢ ⊥ ⊣.

But certain letters, such as H, could not be reversed, and N could not be laid on its side since it would become Z. In these cases the inventor either added something to the letter, or subtracted some portion, so that there could be no ambiguity. The letters thus altered are shown in Fig. 1 (*b*).

But it will probably strike the reader that we have shown alterations of "fixed sounds." We shall explain

Story of Notation

later on, that owing to the possibility of transposing the trope to any semitone of an equally tempered octave, every sound shown in Fig. 1 (a) was capable of becoming either a fixed or movable sound, according to the trope.[1]

The next effort to produce variety resulted in the invention of the Chromatic genus, which remains in use in the Greek Church to the present **The Chro-** day.[2] With Aristoxenus it took three forms: **matic** the *standard chromatic*, consisting of semi- **Tetrachord** tone, semitone, minor third; the *soft chromatic*, in which the two lowest intervals of the tetrachord were

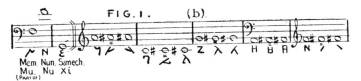

FIG. 1. (b)

Mem. Nun. Samech.
Mu. Nu Xi
(Part of)

⅓ of a tone each; the *sesquialtera chromatic*, in which the first two intervals were ⅜ of a tone. Purists objected to the introduction of the chromatic **The Chro-** genus, which they said had an effeminate **matic Genus** character, and was too voluptuous and **considered** enervating to be good for youth; for one of **effeminate** the chief objects of the cultivation of music

[1] To explain the matter by a modern instance, the note E, for example, is "movable" in the key of C, since it is flattened to produce the key of C minor; but it is "fixed" in the key of D, whether the latter is major or minor.

[2] It can be heard on most Sundays during the Mass at the Greek Church in Bayswater.

The Pycnon

amongst the Greeks was that of education: boys were taught music on account of its humanising influence, just as they are taught Latin and Greek in modern schools, on account of the mental training which is given by a study of these languages.

The same method of notation was used for the chromatic as for the enharmonic genus; The Enharmonic Notation was made to serve for the Chromatic Genus and it is in fact difficult to tell with certainty to which genus any composition that contains the chromatic - enharmonic notation belongs.

EGYPTIAN HARP.

The group of three sounds forming the lower part of the chromatic or enharmonic tetrachord was called "pycnon," *i.e.* "compact," and the pycnon of every tetrachord was noted by the three positions of the letter shown on page 23 and in Fig. 1 (*b*); but the particular tuning used was not shown by the notation.

To a lively people, eager to express their artistic feelings in music, the monotony of a single key would soon become irksome, in spite of the possibility of tuning it in a dozen different ways, and of quarrelling over an equal number of impossible mathematical tunings. They found other outlets for expression in *mode*, and in transposition of the *trope*.

The modes, or better, the octave-species, called by the ancients the harmonies, consisted of certain definite

Story of Notation

orders of tones and semitones, or, in the chromatic
and enharmonic genus, semitones and quarter-tones

**Greek
Harmonies
or Modes**
and ditones or minor thirds, as the cas
might be; and the character of the mus
was much affected by the " harmony " us
for any given composition. Every one
aware that there is a considerable difference of charac
given to modern music according to whether the ma
or the minor mode is used; and that a change fr
minor to major "harmony" will at once attract at

ROMAN LYRE AND KITHARAS.

tion. Instead of our two modes or harmonies, the
Greeks, like their successors the early church musicians,
used seven modes or harmonies, to each of which was
assigned a special character, and was named after the
supposed country of its origin, Dorian, Phrygian,
Lydian, Mixolydian, Hypodorian, Hypophrygian, Hypolydian. There can be only seven octave-species, says
Aristoxenus, for there are only seven sounds in an
octave.

The trope corresponded to our key. We have already

Tropes and Modes

explained on page 16 that the trope consisted of two octaves, containing the greater and the lesser perfect systems: it could commence on any semi-tone of an equally tempered octave, and **The Tropes** there could be modulation both of trope and octave-species in the course of a composition, just as there can be with us a change of key and of mode. The Hymn to Apollo discovered in 1893 at Delphi shows examples of both kinds of change.[1]

It is unfortunate that the Greeks gave the names Dorian, Phrygian, Lydian, etc., to the transpositions of their tropes; and although these trans-positions were intimately connected with the **Confusion** modes, yet much confusion has arisen through **of Terms** the similarity of names: for Boethius, who was held for over a thousand years as the greatest authority on ancient

[1] The following short extract is quoted from the *Bulletin de Correspondance Hellénique*, 1894, p. 588, in which the whole of the " Hymn to Apollo," found engraved on marble by the French School at Delphi, is given, with a translation by Professor Theodore Reinach into modern notation. The rhythm of the music (⅝ time) is shown by the metre of the poetry. Where two or more syllables are to be sung to the same note, the note is not repeated. Where two notes are sung to the same

syllable, its vowel sound is repeated—see το-ος, λοι-οις. The reader will notice the chromatic character of the music, a peculiarity which is still observable in the Greek Church music, though it early disappeared from that of the Western (Roman) Church, which retained the Diatonic genus only.

Story of Notation

music, knowing nothing of transpositions, and mixing up mode and trope, called all the church modes by wrong names. The word Tropos has been usually translated Mode, and this has added to the difficulty. If we could from the first have had the distinction made between trope and octave-species, much useless labour would have been saved. It is usual to refer to the diatonic genus only in describing the modes, since this genus is the only one now known to us; and the keyboard of the organ or piano, which is arranged in accordance with the ancient Greek diatonic tropes, enables us to easily become familiar with the subject.

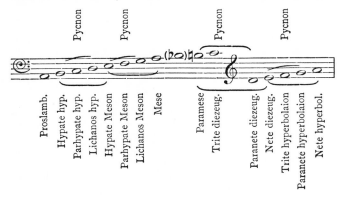

We will quote from two ancient Greek writers. Cleonides, otherwise called Pseudo-Euclid, an Aristoxenian writer, is very clear as to the so-called modes.[1] "Now the species of diapason (*i.e.* octave) are

---

[1] Meibomius, *Euclidis*, Introd. Harmonica, p. 15.

The Common Octave

seven. The first, which is contained between the lower notes of pycna (see page 25), whose first whole tone is at the top, runs from Hypate hypaton to paramese (B to B). It was called by the ancients Mixolydian. The second, which is contained between the middle sounds of pycna, whose whole tone is in the second place from the top, is from Parhypate hypaton to Trite diezeugmenon (C to C). It was called by the ancients Lydian. The third, which is contained between the upper sounds of pycna, whose whole tone is in the third place from the top, runs from Lichanos hypaton to Paranete diezeugmenon (D to D). It was called Phrygian. The fourth, which again is contained between the lower sounds of pycna, whose tone is the fourth from the top, runs from Hypate meson to Nete diezeugmenon (E to E). It was called Dorian. The fifth, contained between the middle sounds of pycna, whose whole tone is in the fifth place from the top, runs as it were from Parhypate meson to Trite hyperbolaion (F to F), and was called Hypolydian. The sixth, between the upper notes of pycna, whose tone is the sixth from the top, runs from Lichanos meson to Paranete hyperbolaion (G to G). It was called Hypophrygian. The seventh, contained between the lower sounds of pycna, whose whole tone has the lowest place, is from Mese to Nete hyperbolaion (A to A) or from Proslambanomenos to mese. It was called Common, or Locrian, or Hypodorian." The reference to the pycna in each case is intended to show that though the tones and semitones were considerably modified by the change of genera, yet the octave-species remained the Dorian or Phrygian as the case might be, as long as the highest and lowest note of the octave was on its proper place in the tetrachord.

The "Common, or Locrian, or Hypodorian" octave (A to A) has given us the starting-point of our modern notation; for, as we shall see later, mediæval musicians, after many experiments, finally settled on calling this octave by the first seven letters of our alphabet.

Boethius, and after him the church musicians for more than 1200 years, mixed the names as follows :—

Story of Notation

Dorian -	-	-	Greek	E to E	Boethius	D to D
Phrygian	-	-	,,	D to D	,,	E to E
Lydian -	-	-	,,	C to C	,,	F to F
Mixolydian	-	-	,,	B to B	,,	G to G

It will be remembered that Bach wrote a Toccata and Fugue in the "Dorian" (D to D) mode, and Beethoven a quartet movement in the "Lydian" (F to F) mode.

We will now turn to Aristoxenus, who tells us[1] that though theoretically there is no limit to the compass of sounds available, yet practically this is limited by voices and instruments to a little over three octaves. "For from the highest sound of the virginal flutes (auloi parthenioi) to the lowest sound of the most perfect flutes (auloi hyperteleioi) may perhaps be a little more than the said three octaves: as may also be the interval from the shortest reed of the pan pipe to the lowest note of the great flute: and likewise the highest sound of a boy's voice to the lowest sound of that of a man."

Here we have definite information that the available compass in the time of Aristoxenus, and probably all through the Roman epoch, was a little over three octaves; and this is borne out by the fifteen tropes of which Alypius gives us the complete notation.

Aristides Quintilianus says[2]: "Let us now speak of Tones. Tone is used in three ways: either for pitch, or for a certain interval produced by the difference between the fourth and the fifth, or for the system of the trope, as the Lydian or Phrygian. And it is of trope that we have to speak here.

"The tones (*i.e.* tropes), according to Aristoxenus, are thirteen in number, and their proslambanomenoi are contained in the diapason (the octave of sounds). But, according to later musicians, there are fifteen tones whose proslambanomenoi extend to the compass of an octave and a tone. And Aristoxenus named them thus: Hypodorius, Hypoiastius, Hypophrygian, Hypoæolian, Hypolydian, Dorian, Iastian, Phrygian, Æolian, Lydian, Hyperdorian, Mixolydian now Hyperiastian, Hypermixolydian or Hyperphrygian. To these the later musicians add two others. . . . And each of the tones is a semi-

---

[1] Meibomius, *Aristox.*, p. 20.   [2] *Ibid.*, p. 22.

Vocal Notation

tone above its predecessor if we begin with the lowest ; but a semitone below its predecessor if we begin with the highest.

"We cannot go lower than the Hypodorian, because its proslambanomenos is the lowest sound that can be heard."

Fortlage[1] calls our scale of A minor the key scale, for by its notation we have a key to the complete notation of the Greeks ; and he made the important discovery that its notation (see Fig. 1, *c*) agrees with the Hypolydian notation given by Alypius. Since Aristoxenus has told us that all the tropes were a semitone apart in the above order, we can from the Hypolydian obtain the relative pitch of all the other tropes, and hence can perfectly well translate their notation into modern notation.

The Modern A Minor Scale has given the Key to the Ancient Notation

FIG. 1.

After the Greeks had perfected their instrumental notation, they invented a new one for the voice. This consisted of their ordinary alphabet, arranged in groups of three letters for the pycna, just as the instrumental notation arranged its single letters in three positions. But here again they did not start, as we should expect, at the top or bottom of the scale : they

Greek Vocal Notation

[1] Fortlage, *Die Musik. System der Griechen*, 1847.

Story of Notation

used Alpha for the sound corresponding to our and proceeded downwards. Completing this alphabet at they started again with a new alpha- bet, of which the letters were inverted or mutilated; while for the sounds above G flat they used a third alphabet, some of whose letters were inverted, while the majority had an acute accent.

The ancient writers who refer to notation invariably give both the vocal and instrumental forms for each note, and we have arranged

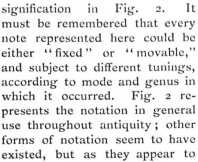

KITHARA.

the complete series of the signs with their modern signification in Fig. 2. It must be remembered that every note represented here could be either "fixed" or "movable," and subject to different tunings, according to mode and genus in which it occurred. Fig. 2 represents the notation in general use throughout antiquity; other forms of notation seem to have existed, but as they appear to

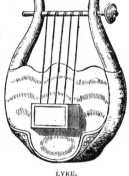

LYRE.

have had only a local and temporary vogue, it is not necessary to discuss them.

CHAPTER III.

The complete scheme of vocal and instrumental notations—Aristoxenus' sarcastic remarks thereon—The conjunct tetrachord suggests modulation to the subdominant—Equal temperament known to the Aristoxenians—Greek notation and equal temperament—Greek rhythmical signs—Some are still in use for teaching Latin—An ancient piece for the aulos, with notation, rhythmical, and accentuation signs, translated into modern notation—The notation of the few existing remnants of Greek music—Greek solmisation—The Christian Church adopted Greek melodies for its hymns, but left off the use of the notation and the instruments—The "Antiphon" of the Roman Church is the successor of the instrumental prelude to Greek songs, the "Alleluia" representing the postlude—Singing schools established — Gregory the Great — Interval between the loss of Greek notation and the invention of a new one—The composition of the gradual and antiphonary—Boethius' so-called notation.

FIGURE 2, p. 34, is a complete scheme of the Greek notation, extracted from the forty-five tables of Alypius; but Aristides gives a few notes below the lowest, and mentions another notation. Such a scheme is called by Aristoxenus a "Catapycnōsis"—*i.e.*, a "scheme of pycna"; and he scoffs violently at those who pretend to teach music from it: for, he says, they seem to think that the notation is the end and object of learning music. The notation, he says, cannot show the

The Complete Notation of Alypius

Story of Notation

exact position of the sounds (this is evident from Fig. 2), and even if it could, no one could sing a series of twenty-eight pycna. Whether he would object to the

FIG. 2.

learning of some of the separate tables as given by Alypius is not known, but he makes it evident that there were many incompetent teachers as well as per-

Order of Tropes

formers in his day. It is beyond the scope of this little book to show how the notation was used for the thirteen tropes, each in the three genera. Those readers who wish to go further into the matter, which is a lengthy one, will find the whole of Alypius' tables laid out in a practical and easily understood form in the first volume of Gevaert's *Histoire de la Musique de l'Antiquité*. The first and third note of each group, when used as proslambanomenoi, are an equal semitone apart. The conjunct tetrachord always adds a flat to its trope—*i.e.*, produces, as we should say, a modulation to the subdominant.[1] Now, if we write out all the tropes in modern notation we shall find that they are exactly expressed by the signatures of our minor scales. Beginning with the " key notation," the Hypolydian, we shall find its intervals expressed by our (descending) scale of A minor. Its conjunct tetrachord introduces B flat, the signature of our scale of D minor—and D minor gives the trope called Lydian. Here the conjunct tetrachord introduces E flat—*i.e.*, a modulation to G minor, which gives the Hyperlydian trope. Here the new flat is A flat, giving the Phrygian trope (C minor). Continuing, we get Hypophrygian, F minor, and its lower octave Hypodorian (also F minor), Dorian, B flat minor, Mixo-

Equal Semitone

Greek Tendency to Modulate to the Subdominant

---

[1] It must not be forgotten that the Greeks had no sign for a flat; to indicate one they were obliged to take the uppermost sign of the pycnon next below the note required to be flattened, or in modern language they had to use A♯ to represent B♭.

35

Story of Notation

lydian, E flat minor, Hypoæolian, A flat or G♯ minor, Æolian, C♯ minor, Hyperæolian, F♯ minor, Iastian, B minor, Hyperiastian, G minor. It is thus

The Complete Circle of Keys known to the Greeks seen that the ancient Greeks made use of the circle of twelve keys, which is supposed to be so modern; and that the inevitable consequence was either theoretical or practical equal temperament, also generally believed to be a modern invention. We have, in the ancient Greek notes of 700 years before the Christian era, a system which is better adapted to that

Greek Notation and Equal Temperament supposed modern innovation, equal temperament, than our own; for whereas we express a semitone in two different ways, as C to C♯, C to D♭, etc.,

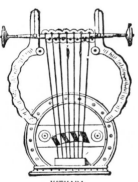

KITHARA.

thus clearly distinguishing between different kinds of semitone, the ancients had a notation which used only one sign for C♯ and D♭, in spite of the fact, which is proved by the writings of Ptolemy and Aristides, that they had exactly the same resources of key at their command as we have on our pianoforte, and that their mathematicians were always insisting on the impossibility of dividing the tone into two equal semitones.

The relative pitch, or interval, between the sounds is

Greek Rules of Composition

not the only thing that a notation is required to express; for mere melody without rhythm and accent is formless and meaningless. The ancient Greeks laid even more stress on the theory of rhythm than we do, and Aristoxenus wrote a whole book about it.

Every melody was intimately connected with its words, in ways that we should consider intensely artificial. In the first place, certain syllables were obliged to have higher notes than their neighbours, and certain diphthongs were provided with two notes; and in the second place, the rhythm of the melody was note for note dependent on the metre of the words: so that a long syllable was sung to a long note, and a short syllable to a short note; and a so-called long syllable was really pronounced long, *i.e.*, dwelt upon. Some idea may perhaps be got of the effect of such dwelling upon a syllable by observing the somewhat sing-song method in which the modern Italian dwells on those portions of words that precede double consonants, such as morēl-la, cavāl-lo, Giovān-ni, etc. No time-signs were therefore necessary to a musician familiar with the scansion of poetry; but for instrumental music, and for doubtful

Vocal Melody

EGYPTIAN STRINGED INSTRUMENT.

cases, certain signs were placed over the notes to indicate their duration. They are given by an anonymous Greek writer of about A.D. 200, but they were in use long before his time.

37

Story of Notation

The short syllable produced a single "time" in the music, or, as we might say, a quaver; and whatever **Time-signs** the value of the "time" given by the first short syllable, that "time" remained the measure for the rest of the piece.

Grammarians used the sign ∪ to indicate a short syllable, and continue to do so to this day; but musicians used no sign for it. The time-signs used by musicians, and given by Anonymus, are the long, or two-time short, indicated thus —, equivalent to a crotchet, ♩ The three-time long was indicated thus ∟, equivalent to a dotted crotchet, ♩. The four-time long, shown thus ⊔, was equivalent to a minim, ♩ The five-time long, ⊔⊔, was equivalent to ♩♪

Accent was shown by a dot called ictus, placed above the note, but the ictus occurs irregularly, just as does the modern bar-line in the first half of the seventeenth century.

Rests, called empty times, were shown thus:—

Rests

        Single-time rest, ∧, equivalent to   ⅎ

        Two-time rest, ⊼,   ,,   Ɛ̄

        Three-time rest, ⌐⊼,   ,,   Ɛ̄ⅎ

        Four-time rest, ⊔⊣⊼,   ,,   ▬

The anonymous writer gives the notation of a number of vocal exercises, sung to the syllables to-a, ta-e, te-o, pairs of slurred notes, the slur being shown by joining the notes thus, ⌒ᴗ.

Ancient Melodies

The sign **X** between two notes appears to have indicated that the first was to be sung *staccato*.[1]

There are also in this tract several instrumental exercises, in which the time and accent are clearly marked over the notes. The following little piece is supposed to be for the aulos:—

The Greek notation had a vogue of about a thousand years; the enharmonic and chromatic genera fell out of general use, though every theorist felt bound to describe them. "Anonymus" tells us that the players of different instruments made use of different modes and tropes: thus the players of hydraulic organs used six of the tropes, the kitharists four, the flute players seven, the musicians who accompanied the dance seven; and he gives lists of the modes used by each. The various exercises for voice and flute given by him, and the three well-known Hymns to Apollo, Nemesis, and the Muse, are all in the Lydian (D minor) trope.[2] The Hymn to Apollo found at Delphi in 1893 begins in the Phrygian (C minor) and ends in the Hyperphrygian (F minor) trope. Both parts contain accidentals borrowed from other tropes. There are fragments of

Duration of the Greek Notation

Existing Examples in the Ancient Notation

---

[1] Bellermann, Anonymus, p. 25.   [2] Appendix A, "Galileo."

Story of Notation

another Delphic hymn in the Lydian trope, and with instrumental notation : the instrumental notation seems to have been frequently used for voices. A fragment of a chorus from the *Orestes* of Euripides, discovered on a papyrus and published in 1892 at Vienna, is in the Lydian trope, and contains an independent instrumental accompaniment ; but it is too mutilated to give any idea of its effect. Two other fragments are known—a piece of the music of Pindar's first Pythic ode, given by Kircher, of doubtful authenticity, though it obeys all the known rules of Greek composition.[1] It is in the Phrygian trope, and contains both vocal and instrumental signs.—A fragment of music discovered at Tralles, carved on a pillar, is in the Iastian (B minor) notation. As this music is supposed to date from the second century of our era, it shows that the Lydian trope, though most general, was not the only one used at that time.

Besides the letter notation, the Greeks, under the Roman Empire, and perhaps earlier, used a system of solmisation for singing exercises, consisting **Greek** of the syllables τω, τα, τη, τε, to the four **Solmisa-** notes of the tetrachord ; and τωννω, ταννα, **tion** τηννη, τεννε. These syllables are given only by "Anonymus," who quotes a number of examples

---

[1] The notation of part of Pindar's first Pythic ode is thus given in Kircher's *Musurgia*. Kircher says that he found the original MS. in the monastery of San Salvator at Messina; but no traces of it have been discovered by the numerous antiquarians who have searched for it since his day. The modern notation is, of course, not found in Kircher.

40

A Melody by Pindar

FIG. 2 A.
Chorus Vocalis.

Chorus Instrumentalis.

Story of Notation

with notation to show how they are to be used—
thus :

and similar exercises, such as a singing-master would
use now.

By the sixth century A.D. Greek notation was known
only through the works of theorists, which were no
longer understood, and a new one had not yet
been invented. The early Christian Church
seems to have adapted the popular Lyrodes
(songs with the lyre) to its use, just as in later
times Martin Luther adapted secular tunes
for the purposes of his Reformation. Arius, the heretic,
in order to attract the multitude, made use of the tunes
composed by Sotades, an Ionian poet, who
was notorious for the lasciviousness of his
songs; and the orthodox bishops combated
his heresy by writing hymns in Syriac to the
same tunes.[1] But the greatest musician
of this early period was St. Ambrose of Milan, who was
accused of fascinating the people with the
charm of the hymns he composed as an
antidote to heresy. He is known to have been
the composer and author of at least six hymns at present
in use in the Church, and he was probably the author

Disappearance of Greek Music

Secular Tunes used to combat Heresy

St. Ambrose of Milan

[1] Gevaert, *Hist. de la Mus. de l'Antiquité*, vol. iii. pp. 63, 65, etc.

Ambrosian Music

of four others. He was followed by Prudentius, a poet whose songs for solo voice and lyre were intended for home singing by the Christians in place of the hymns addressed to pagan deities. After his time hymn composition fell into the hands of priests and monks and inferior poets, who continued all through the Middle Ages to compose more or less correct Ambrosian tunes.[1]

Prudentius

How were these Ambrosian hymns handed down? We hear and read little of them, for the Roman or Gregorian Church music has overshadowed the Ambrosian, which is practically confined to Milan. The music appears to have been entirely empirical. The lyre and flute were rigidly excluded from the basilicas of the Christians, since they were connected with the hated pagan worship. The place of the introductory prelude, called Crouma, which was intended to give the pitch and to remind the singer of the tune, was taken by the antiphon, sung by the priest, and the postlude was represented by the Alleluia. The instrumental notation was not therefore any longer required.

Gaudentius, who seems to have lived towards the end of the fifth century A.D., says that " the ancients made use of certain letters intended to show musical notes." It appears, then, that the use of the notation had practically ceased by his time, and that after Theodosius had closed the pagan schools, the notation was no longer taught. The *répertoire* of Christian

Greek Notation referred to as a thing of the past

[1] Gevaert, vol. iii. pp. 78, 79.

43

Story of Notation

music was extending, singing schools were opened, but as yet everything was taught by ear.

Singers went out into distant countries from the singing schools to teach, but we hear of no kind of nota-**Singing taught by Ear** tion until the beginning of the eighth century. Christianity introduced two new things into its music: the rhyme, and the singing of the prose words of Scripture. The rhyme was invented in the early days, and was used to attract the vulgar; and the setting of prose words to music was a novelty unknown to the ancient Greeks, who only sang poetry.

It is related by John the Deacon that Gregory the Great, who was Pope from A.D. 590 to 604, collected the sacred music of the Church and had it written in a book called the *Antiphonary,* which was chained to the altar of St. Peter's as a model of what the music should be; that

MUSICIANS. (FROM EGYPTIAN SLABS.)

44

Gregory the Great

he founded the school of singing at Rome, that he himself taught the boys, and that in the ninth century there were still shown the couch on which he lay while teaching during illness, and the rod with which he beat the scholars. Much doubt has been thrown on this story, since it is not mentioned by any contemporary writer or by the Venerable Bede, who lived in the next century and wrote much upon the music of the Liturgy; and the only allusion in the writings of Gregory himself to music is a decree of 595, that the singers who were priests were not to occupy themselves only with singing, which merely delighted the people, while it irritated God, but were to lead a life of edification, to confine the use of their voices to the recitation of the Gospel, and to leave the singing to the subdeacons and inferior clergy. This does not point to Gregory the Great having been favourable to the music of the Liturgy, and it was probably a later Pope Gregory who organised it.[1] Moreover, if the old Greek notation was no longer used, and a new one was not invented till the eighth century, it seems impossible that Gregory the Great could have written the music in a book, even if he had collected it.

Gevaert, from an exhaustive analysis of the Gregorian Chant, places the composition of the whole of the Antiphonary and Gradual and Hymns between the years A.D. 425 and 700. He divides this period

Legend of Gregory the Great

Gregory was no friend of music

[1] Gevaert, *Origines du Chant Liturgique*, 1890, pp. 19, etc.

Story of Notation

into two epochs : the first, the epoch of simple or
syllabic chant, in which one note (or at most two)

Probable Date of Composition of Gradual and Antiphonary
was sung to each syllable, he places during the last years of the Western Empire, and the Gothic supremacy at Rome. This kind of chant is a direct inheritance from, or adaptation of, Greek music.

The second period is that of the florid chant, which was cultivated to a very high degree of perfection in the singing schools. This epoch he places at the time of the domination of the Byzantine emperors at Rome, from A.D. 555 onwards ; and during that period the notation by neumes began to be used.[1]

Boethius, like Gaudentius, refers to the Greek notation as a thing of the past. "The ancient musicians, in order to facilitate reference, and to avoid the necessity of always quoting strings by their full names, invented certain little notes (*notulas*) by which the names of the strings were noted and divided into their genera and modes, with such brevity that if any one wished to describe a melody, he could write it above the verse ; and these notes of sounds were so admirably made that not only the words, but also the melody, could be handed down to posterity," etc. It is evident from the above that the Greek notation had fallen out of common use, and Boethius himself, after giving a description of the Lydian notation, does not use it for his examples, but employs the Latin alphabet, not

[1] *Origines du Chant Liturgique,* pp. 21, etc.

46

An Unorthodox Notation

in the consecutive order of the
scale, but, as Euclid does, mere-
Boethius'   ly to indicate points
Use of   to which he is refer-
Latin   ring; so that, for ex-
Letters to   ample, A refers in one
indicate   place to proslambano-
Sounds   menos, in another to
hypate, etc. The origin of
the Latin lettering of the
scale cannot therefore be
referred to Boethius, who
neither invented nor used
any kind of notation.

Before concluding this
chapter, we must mention
another notation referred to
by David and Lussy.[1] The
tetrachords are divided into
ten quarter-tones, to which
are applied the first ten letters of
An Un-   the Greek alphabet,
orthodox   which recommences
Greek   with each new ascend-
Notation   ing tetrachord, as our
alphabet recommences with each
new octave. This notation has
been found in one MS. only,

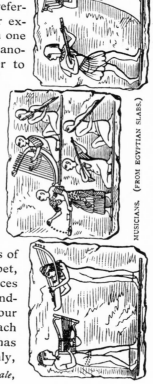

MUSICIANS. (FROM EGYPTIAN SLABS.)

[1] *Histoire de la Notation Musicale,*
1882, p. 27.

Story of Notation

connected with the work of Aristides Quintilianus. It is nowhere else referred to; it ascends the scale, whereas we know that the Greeks practised their scales from the top downwards, not as we do from the bottom upwards; it is absolutely methodical and complete, each new tetrachord having a second letter attached to each of the ten letters. All this, in our opinion, points to its being either a very late invention which was never adopted, or a mere reference scheme for the use of the writer and reader, as we have seen was the case with the so-called Boethian notation.

CHAPTER IV.

The development of the neumes out of the Greek accents—An early codex of Virgil's works, with neumes—The neumatic notation— The Romanian signs—Free Rhythm—Difference between *neuma*, a sign, and *pneuma*, a breathing—Explanation of the means adopted by the Benedictines of Solesmes to decipher the neumes— Mistakes exposed by their researches—The liquescents indicate a *nuance*, which can be observed in the singing of untrained village choirs of to-day—The modern letter notation derived from the monochord—Gregory the Great could not have invented it—Other attempts to invent a letter notation—The rise of *organum*—Early efforts to invent a pictorial notation—Influence of Greek learning on Hucbald—Line and dot notations found in Sicily—Attempts to combine phonetic and pictorial notations.

As long as the schools of singing at Rome were flourishing, as long as the teachers were enthusiastic, and the music of the Church was young and vigorous, it was possible to hand down the melodies by ear from master to pupil, and from generation to generation. The possibilities of correct transmission by memory, where no system of writing is known, are surprising. The Homeric poems were recited and handed down for generations before they were written; and, to take a more modern instance, the Maories of New Zealand were some twenty years ago, and possibly are now, able to recite from memory their genealogical trees,

Music handed down to succeeding generations by Memory

Story of Notation

reaching back for 500 years, the art of writing having been unknown to them till taught by the English missionaries. But with the spread of the Church, and the increasing demand for teachers, the necessity arose of some

NEUME NOTATION. (TENTH CENTURY.)

Per - fi-ce gres - sus me - os   in se - mi -tis tu - is.

TRANSLATION OF NEUMES, AFTER SOLESMES.

means of at any rate reminding the singer of the tunes he had learned; and this necessity produced a new form of indicating melody, which has developed into our staff notation.

The keen-witted Greeks had not failed to perceive that in ordinary speaking, and especially in rhetorical utterance, the voice rises and falls. Aristo-

Modern Notation developed from Greek Accents
xenus calls these inflections " continuous melody," as opposed to "systematic movement," by the fixed intervals of musical " systems." Now, the grammarians indicated the rise and fall of the speaking voice by accents—*accentus* from *ad cantus*, " belonging to the song,"—not the song of definite intervals, but the melody

Accents and Melody

of the speaking voice, called "continuous melody." The Greek word for accent is *prosōdia,* which originally meant an accompanied song;[1] thus both the Greek and Latin form of the word show the intimate connection of "accent" with melody. It must be borne in mind that only with the decline of Greek music and literature and art, did the use of accents begin—they were simply intended to remind the reader of what he had learned with regard to the inflections of his voice.

The three accents used for this purpose were the acute, in which the pen makes a stroke rising from **The Three Accents indicating the rise and fall of the voice** left to right, showing that the voice has to rise; the grave, in which the pen, by falling from left to right, indicates a fall of the voice; and the circumflex, indicating a fall on a single syllable. This theory of the Greek accents has received a remarkable confirmation within recent years by the discoveries at Delphi. The syllables which bear acute accents are invariably given higher notes than their neighbours,

[1] Liddell & Scott Lexicon, 7th edition.

GOTHIC NOTATION.

Story of Notation

while the syllables with circumflex accents have a descent of two, or even three notes.

At some time or other, it is not known when, the teachers of Gregorian music began to make use of the Greek accents as *memoriæ technici* for the melody. But they went further. Having once grasped the idea that a rising accent gave a picture of a rising sound, a falling accent of a falling sound, they elaborated a complete system of notation called neumatic. It is an interesting fact that the earliest codex of the works of Virgil, one of the chief treasures of the Laurentian Library at Florence, and which dates from the fourth century, is provided with neumes, as a guide to the reader or reciter; but the different colour of the ink shows that they are of a later date than the book. There is a facsimile copy of this codex in the British Museum, but the editor, evidently not understanding the neumes, has omitted them altogether.

The earliest existing MS. of Virgil's Works

At what date the use of the accents of the grammarians to remind singers of what they had learned by ear began is not known. It is supposed to be of Byzantine origin, and there are traces of it in the notation still used by the Greek Church, as we shall show later (page 194). We find the Antiphonary provided with complete and fully developed neumatic notation, dating from the ninth century, in the Library of St. Gall; and the use of this notation was known all over Europe at that time. Not only so, but the

The Neumes

St. Gall MSS. contain marks of expression invented by Romanus, a monk of St. Gall, such as l. *levatur,* higher, iu. *jusum,* lower, c. *celeriter,* quickly, b.t. *bene tene,* our *tenuto.* The "Romanian letters" were continued in many MSS. till the thirteenth century.

Marks of Expression found in the earliest Neumatic MSS.

The groups of notes were all given names, which have been preserved in various mediæval writings ; and the shapes of the neumes varied with different handwritings and in different countries, though they were always easy to recognise. Unfortunately, they were merely a guide to those who were already familiar with the melodies: they indicated where the voice went up and down, but gave no clue to the interval to be sung, whether a semitone or tone or third or fourth or fifth, etc., so that they are useless to those who are not previously

The Neumes could not indicate Intervals

familiar with the music. Neither did they indicate the value of notes; for the idea of fixing the length of prose syllables by means of measured notes had not yet occurred to musicians. The words were sung as pronounced, except where a number of notes or a pneuma occurred, in which case the syllable was lengthened to suit the tune ; but the fixed rhythm of crotchets and quavers, etc., as applied to prose, was as yet unknown. " Free Rhythm," in which groups of notes and

Free Rhythm

words are sung without definite time value, is well indicated by the neumatic notation, and it is impossible to represent Free Rhythm by means of modern notation.

The word *neuma* (a sign) must not be confounded with *pneuma* (a breathing), as several writers have

Neuma and Pneuma done. The latter, it is true, is a kind of accent used over a vowel in the places where we should use the letter H : but in the neumatic notation *pneuma* means a long florid passage, sung on one syllable, or even with no syllable at all ; an outcome of religious fervour so intense that it could no longer express itself by words, but by melody alone. The meaning and proper execution of the *pneumata* being misunderstood in the sixteenth century, they were curtailed or suppressed by Palestrina in his edition of the Gradual, which is used at the present day in the Roman Church.

Are the neumes capable of solution? A few years ago this question was answered in the negative, in

How the Neumes have been solved spite of the labours of many learned men. But since the monks of the Benedictine monastery of Solesmes have called photography to their aid, they have succeeded in deciphering all the more important MSS. containing the music of the Gradual and Antiphonary, except that the interpretation of two of the ornamental neumes is still somewhat doubtful. Fig. 3 is intended to show the process by which the solution has been arrived at. It is, of course, by no means exhaustive ; it gives only a few of the many combinations of grave and acute accent, and the number of columns might be extended

FIG. 3.

FIG. 3.	ORIGINAL FORM	ST GALL XI CENT.	GERMANY XII CENT.	CAMBRAI XII CENT.	ITALY XII CENT.	GOTHIC A.D. 1260.	GOTHIC A.D. 1563.	SARUM GRADUAL XIII CENT	ITALY A.D. 1480.
VIRGA.	/	ſ	ʃ	⋀	l	℘	₤	ꟼ	ꟼ
PUNCTUM.	•	—	—	⋏	—	◆	◆	▱	▱◆
CLIVIS.	⋀	⋒	⋔	⅂	⋔	⋔	⋔	⅃	⅃
PODATUS.	⌣	⌣	⌣	⌣	⌐	⅃	◄	⅃	⅃
SCANDICUS SALICUS.	⦙	⦙	⅃	⦙	⊣	⁙	⁙	⅃	⅃
CLIMACUS.	⋰	⋰	⋰	⋰	⊢	℘⋰	℘⋰	ꟼ⋰	ꟼ⋰
TORCULUS	⋀	⋒	♪	⋒	⋀	⋀	♫	⋔	⋔
PORRECTUS.	⋁	⋁	⋁	Ⅴ	⋁	⋒	⋒	⋈	⋈
PODATUS SUBPUNCTIS.	⌣⋰	⌣⋰	⅃⋰	⌣⋰	⊣⋰	⅃⋰	⅃⋰	⅃⋰	⅃⋰
CLIMACUS RESUPINUS.	⋰⌣	⋰⌣	⋰⌣	⋰⌣		⋰⌣	⋰⌣	ꟼ⋰⌣	ꟼ⋰⌣
SCANDICUS FLEXUS.	♪	Ⅱ		⋔	⊐⋀			♪	♫
SCANDICUS SUBPUNCTIS.	⋰⋰	⋰⋰	⋰⋰	⋰⋰	⊣⋰	⁙⋰	⁙⋰	⅃⋰	⅃⋰
TORCULUS RESUPINUS.	⋌⋁	⋌⋁		⋈		⋈	⋈	⋈	⋈
PORRECTUS FLEXUS.	⋈	⋈	⋁	⅃				⅃	⋈
PORRECTUS SUBPUNCTIS.	⋁⋰	⋁⋰	⋁⋰	⋈⋰	⋁⋰			⋈⋰	⋈⋰

1 2 3 4 5 6 7 8 9

55

indefinitely. Still, it will answer for purposes of explanation.

The *Virga* or *Virgula, Anglice* rod, the acute accent, indicates a note higher than its neighbours.
Names of the Neumes This is strikingly exemplified in the recent discoveries of Greek music.

The *Punctum*, point, is undoubtedly equivalent to the grave or descending accent, though this does not occur in the neumes.

The *Clivis* or *Clinis* is a combination of acute and grave accent—it is the circumflex accent, indicating a high followed by a low note.

The *Podatus* or *Pes* is named from its shape—a foot. It is a punctum joined to a virga—*i.e.,* a lower followed by a higher note.

Scandicus, Salicus, Latin words meaning climber—an ascent of two or more points and a virga.

Climacus, little ladder, a high note followed by two or more lower ones.

Torculus, twisted—low, high, low.

Porrectus, extended—high, low, high.

The rest of the neumes given in Fig. 3 are merely modifications of those already explained, and can be easily understood; the number of possible combinations was very great, but all can be understood from the few given.

Thus much was always known about the neumes; what was not known was how high or how low the sounds represented by them were with regard to one another. Did a clivis represent an interval of a semi-

Benedictine Research

tone, a tone, a third, fourth, and so on? and the same of the podatus. Did the scandicus and climacus represent successive scale sounds or leaps? and what were its intervals? These questions, which puzzled the learned men of the present day, also troubled the ancients, and in course of time they drew lines across the page as a guide. The idea took root, and in a short time the stave was invented, after which the intervals were definitely known.

The Benedictines of Solesmes hit on the happy idea of making thousands of photographs from the MSS. of the Gradual and Antiphonary in all the libraries in Europe, and a comparison of these *The process of unravelling the Neumes* photographs revealed a most remarkable similarity in the neumes and in the notes of the various countries of Western Europe. The traditional melodies had been preserved with the most scrupulous care: the notes of later times and the neumes of earlier times were found to agree in almost every particular; and whether a gradual or an antiphon was sung in Italy or Spain or England, whether it was sung in the ninth century or in the fifteenth, its melody was the same.[1] Now it is easy enough to read the square or Gothic notation, columns 6 to 9, Fig. 3, since it is always written on a stave; and by the simple process of comparing an antiphon written in square notation, with the same antiphon

---

[1] The agreement amongst the MSS. is so remarkable that the Benedictines are inclined to attribute it to miraculous interposition, and the melodies themselves to divine inspiration.

Story of Notation

written in neumes, we easily arrive at the interpretation of the neumes for that particular antiphon ; and we can continue this process till a whole book is translated. As a matter of fact, the square notation of Plainsong is a translation of the neumes.

The Benedictines have eliminated several old-established errors. In the first place the virga never indicated **Errors exposed** a long note, but merely a high note, though it is occasionally used for low notes. The virga of columns 8 and 9 therefore is no longer or shorter than the punctum of columns 6, 7, and 9. The neumes have nothing to do with the time values of later measured music, in which the square-headed virga was double or three times the value of the lozenge-shaped punctum. Secondly, it is sometimes thought that the form of the neumes and of the Gothic notation changed at specified periods. Comparison of many manuscripts has shown that this was not the case. The older unstaved neumatic notation continued to be used for centuries after the lines had been invented ; and columns 6 and 7 show that the awkward early Gothic forms were used for centuries after the invention of the square notation, as shown in columns 8 and 9. The shapes shown in Fig. 3 are taken at random from amongst the hundreds of photographs published in the *Paléographie Musicale* at Solesmes.

Column 1 shows the usual forms in the earlier MSS. In column 2 we see the commencement of the tendency to place a head on the virga. The

58

Neumatic Notation

origin of the head was in the action of the pen in rapid writing: it was drawn upwards, and a slight involuntary pressure given as it left the parchment, and the resulting slight enlargement afterwards took the forms shown in columns 2, 3, 4, 7, until it became stereotyped in the square head of columns 8 and 9. **The addition of a Head to the Virga**

The various shapes of the punctum are also due to the same cause. A broad-nibbed pen drawn downwards the shortest possible distance from left to right (the grave accent) produced the lozenge of columns 6, 7, 9.

The clivis throughout preserves its virga, followed by its lower note.

The podatus is simply a lower note joined to a virga.

The scandicus alters in the Sarum Gradual (column 8) to a podatus and a virga, but in later MSS. is found in its original form (column 9). The porrectus became the ligature of measured music, and as such gave more trouble to both ancient and modern theorists than the whole of the rest of the notation. The oblique line always represents two sounds, namely, those of the lines or spaces on which it begins and ends. In the notation of Plainsong the ligature has of course no time value; but in measured music its time value is exceedingly difficult to unravel.

We have not space here to give a full description of the neumatic notation, for this interesting subject is very far reaching, but we must mention some of the

Story of Notation

other neumes. They are the *Apostropha* (ʼ), the *Distropha* (ʼ ʼ), and the *Tristropha* (ʼ ʼ ʼ). These indicate repeated sounds.

The *Strophicus* and *Oriscus* and *Pressus* are slightly different forms of the above, with slightly different meanings.

The *Quilisma*, a sign something like our indication of a shake, occurs between the lower and upper notes of an ascending minor third. It is supposed to have been a kind of tremolo.

The *Epiphonus*, a kind of shortened podatus, and the *Cephalicus*, a modification of the clivis, were "liquescents." The Solesmes photographs show that these neumes were used in connection with the "half vowels" or "liquescent" letters L, M, N, R, in which the sound is carried on to the succeeding consonant.

The *Ancus* is a virga or podatus with a rounded head. It is also called *pes cornutus*—horned foot, and several other names. It has to do with the liquescent letters. Perhaps the liquescent notes arose from a practice which can be observed in uneducated country choir singers of the present day, who sometimes carry a syllable into the succeeding note, thus:—

All peo-ple that on earth do dwell.

But though the neumes were the ordinary means of reminding singers of the rise and fall of the melodies they had learned by heart, there were in existence letter

The Monochord

notations as well, though they were not much used for
singing at sight. They were derived from the monochord, an instrument of one long string,   Latin
which was measured off by a movable   Alpha-
bridge, the bridge being placed at certain   betical
points called A, B, C, D, etc., to pro-   Notations
duce the various notes. The old enhar-   coeval
monic and chromatic scales, and the various   with the
tunings of the diatonic scale had long dis-   Neumes
appeared, as well as the whole of the system of transposition of tropes. One trope only remained, the original
shown in Fig. 1 (c), and this was made the foundation
of the divisions of the monochord. These divisions were
very early indicated by the letters of the Latin alphabet.

It was found that by taking away the bridge altogether the whole string gave a sound lower than A;
and as both forms of the Latin G had
been taken for sounds above A, the Greek   A Note
letter gamma was taken to represent this   added below
low sound: hence our word gamut,[1] and the   Proslamba-
French word *gamme,* meaning scale. Here,   nomenos
then, was a definite fixing of the intervals for teaching
purposes at any rate, and though many attempts were
made to utilise the letter notation for reading   Attempts to
music at sight, yet, fortunately for us, none   read Music
of them succeeded, or the staff notation   by Phonetic
might perhaps never have been invented.   Notation
The use of the first seven letters of the   fail

[1] " The gamut is the ground and foundation of music."—Playford,
Rules for Song, 1658.

61

Story of Notation

Gregory
the Great
did not
invent the
Modern
Letter
Notation
alphabet in music has until quite recently been always ascribed to Gregory the Great; but Gevaert points out that he could not have been its inventor, since the first to use it systematically was Guido of Arezzo, who did not live till some four centuries later. From the time of Guido it has been accepted by all Western musicians, and has remained in use to this day, though the Greek gamma only remains in the word gamut.

Various
attempts
to apply
the Latin
Alphabet
for pur-
poses of
Notation
Many other attempts were made to apply the letters of the Latin alphabet to the greater perfect system of the Greeks. Gevaert mentions six :—

1. An anonymous writer of a treatise called *De Harmonica Institutione* suggests the following method, thus recognising the major mode as the fundamental scale :—

A B C D E F G   A B C D E F G &c.

2. A notation composed of various forms and positions of the letter F, to be described below.

3. A notation in which, starting from proslamba-nomenos, which is called A (as in our system), all the intervals of the chromatic and enharmonic scales are lettered with Latin letters on the plan of the catapycnosis, Fig. 2, the alphabet proceeding upwards instead of down

62

Early Experiments

the scale. This is given by Adelbold, a contemporary of Hucbald.[1]

4. Starting from proslambanomenos as A, the alphabet proceeds to L, which is our d, the end of the lesser perfect system ; then, starting again with M, our B♮, it proceeds to S, our aa. This is suggested by an anonymous writer, before Guido Aretino.

5. Starting from proslambanomenos as A, the alphabet proceeds as far as P, our aa, taking no notice of B♭. This is derived from Boethius.

6. Towards the end of the eleventh century an anonymous writer suggests the same notation as the Guidonian —*i.e.,* Γ, A, B, C, etc., but above G he begins the Greek alphabet, in no regular order.

It would seem, then, that there were as many attempts made in these early days to improve the notation as there are at present; for we may be sure that the six or seven systems which have come down to us represent many others that have been lost. Nowadays, when there is absolutely no need for it, we get a "new and improved" notation, which is intended to supersede the staff notation, about once every two or three years; and all these attempts, after being carefully catalogued, sink into oblivion on the shelves of the British Museum.

Ten centuries ago there was a pressing necessity for a new notation. Music was advancing, and the old methods were not adequate to record it: new schools were being founded, new compositions made, and it

[1] About A.D. 900.

Story of Notation

was necessary to teach at Paris what was composed at Rome, or to sing at Madrid the music produced at Winchester. In the twentieth century we have a universally accepted notation, and music composed in Rome can be performed in Paris within two days of its publication, owing to the labours of mediæval musicians. Yet in spite of this, human nature is such, that men are as anxious now to improve or supersede the staff notation as they were to invent it in the tenth century. The

A Single Example in which Phonetic and Pictorial Notations are combined two systems of indicating the pitch of sound were then in use concurrently, the phonetic and the pictorial; but only in one single manuscript, the famous Montpellier Antiphonary, were they combined. And if we come to consider what the neumes meant, it was perhaps not so strange that our forefathers were a long time in seeking a satisfactory combination. The neumes were

signs indicating such delicate shades of accent and rhythm, and such flowing and spontaneous melodies, that it would seem as impossible to represent them by bare and cold-looking letters as it is to represent them by modern notation, in which the note values are mathematically proportioned to one another. Hence, though many attempts were made, yet none succeeded for many generations.[1]

[1] We were once asked by a naturalist whether it was possible to record in writing the song of birds—*e.g.*, the nightingale. The only attempt we know of is that made by Kircher in his *Musurgia*, by means of musical notation, which, of course, is totally inadequate for

The Organum

Somewhere about the ninth century men began to make practical use of the "symphonies" and "dia-phonies" (concords and discords) of the old Greek writers—*i.e.,* they began to sing in parts. It is true that the parts they sang in were at first a rigorous adaptation of the "symphonies" only to the plainsong; in other words, they sang in nothing but consecutive fifths, and fourths, and octaves; but this kind of singing, which, "if sung by two or more voices, with suitable slowness, you will see that it produces a sweet concord,"[1] imperatively demanded fixation of the intervals. It has sometimes been debated whether such music could ever have been tolerated, and some years ago we heard a university professor deliver a lecture, in which he endeavoured to prove that the so-called "organum" never existed in anything but theory. But in an early stage of musical culture these intervals are just the ones that come most naturally to the front; and the word used by Hucbald for concord is *con-centum,* singing together. Many musicians heard in the late 'eighties the "unemployed" of London walking about the streets and singing; the tenors pitched their voices at a fifth above the basses, and sang the tune with them quite happily. This was the ancient organum pure and simple.

Rise of Singing in Parts

The "Organum" heard in London Streets

the purpose. If the song of birds is ever capable of being recorded, it will be by some such system as the neumatic notation of the Early Fathers.

[1] Hucbald, *Enchiriadis,* in Gerbert, vol. i. p. 166.

Story of Notation

Another instance occurred within our own experience: a party of Christmas waits in Rutland sang "Adeste Fideles" with a violin in unison, while a clarionettist,

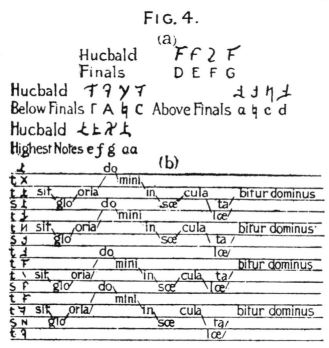

FIG. 4.

who could play only in one key, played the tune quite unconcernedly a fourth above the singers.

Our chief information on the organum of the ninth

Hucbald and Odo

and tenth centuries is derived from the *Musica Enchiriadis*, ascribed to Hucbald, a monk of St. Amand in Flanders, a very learned man, who died at a great age in A.D. 930 or 940, but now supposed to be by Odo, an Abbot of Tomières. The writer, whoever he may have been, **"Musica Enchiriadis"** was very much wedded to the old Greek learning, as exhibited in the work of Boethius, and wished to make all music of his time conform to it. Hence he resuscitated the old long-winded names,[1] and gave Latin letters to them, such as I to Mese, M to Lichanos meson, P to Parhypate meson, C to Hypate meson, etc., and wrote the letters over the words that were to be sung, as in the old Greek manner, an idea which he evidently derived from Boethius' casual use of the Latin letters. But this system did not succeed, and he tried others. Taking the finals of the four Church modes as his basis, he indicated them by the letter F in different forms—Fig. 4 (*a*). He then, in accordance with Greek precedent, inverted and mutilated the letter for the sounds above and below the final; for the sounds above aa **Notation by the Letter F** he was not able to invent notes, and Odo of Clugny calls them "remaining" (superfluous) sounds. He gives in his *Short Memoir on the Singing of the Tones and the Psalms* many pages of psalms adapted to this notation, and finally a page of neumes connected with it. It is referred to again by Hermann Contractus, who suggests as an alternative the letters E for unison,

[1] Vide *Ambros Geschichte*, Band 2, pp. 122 *et seq.*

Story of Notation

S for semitone, T for tone, TS for minor third (tone and semitone), TT major third, D for fourth, Δ for fifth, ΔS minor sixth, ΔT major sixth, ΔD octave. But both these clumsy systems also failed; in fact, they had no possible advantage over placing the ordinary Latin letters above the notes, the objection to which we have seen.

FIG. 4 (c).

Pictorial Notation suggested by Hucbald.

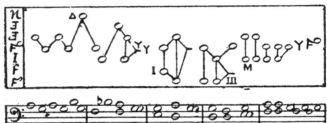

The writer of *Enchiriadis* now invented a new notation, and this may possibly have been the parent of our staff. He drew lines, wrote at the beginning **The First Line Notation** ning T for tone and S for semitone, and wrote the words between the lines, adding the various forms of F to show the pitch, and joining the syllables by lines to guide the eye. Fig. 4 (*b*), which gives a complete scheme of organum in four parts, in fourths, fifths, and octaves, is perhaps the earliest existing example of a full score. This

A Sicilian Notation

systom also failed, and men continued to use the neater
and more familiar neumes.

Many other attempts were made to invent a practicable notation. Galilei and Kircher refer to a system
of which they found traces, wherein points
were placed on lines ; and Kircher says he
found it in a MS. of the tenth century. If
he is right, it dates from the time of Hucbald.
He gives in vol. i., p. 213, the example shown in Fig. 5 (*a*),
and says that he found many hymns written with music
in this way in the library of the monastery of San

Another
Line
Notation

FIG. 5.
(a)

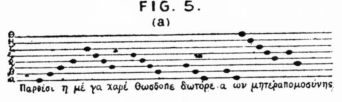

Salvator at Messina, the same library, by the way, in
which he discovered the Greek music of Pindar's first
Pythic Ode. The lines only are used, and the notes are
shown by "black points, or rather little circles." The
spaces are unoccupied, and at the beginning of the
eight lines are eight Greek letters which are quite incomprehensible, for, as Ambros points out, they accom-
modate themselves to no known system of notation.

But Galilei is more explicit. He says that before the
time of Guido the points were placed on seven lines,
which were lettered according to the Greek heptachord

Story of Notation

of Terpander (Fig. 5, *b*).[1] Notice how these early musicians could never get away from the Greek teaching. Galilei tries to show that the system he describes was once in general use, but Ambros points out that if this had been the case we must have

FIG. 5. **(b)**

heard more about it. May it not have been used in some remote locality? The present writer, many **Local Notations** years ago, came across a local system of musical notation which had been used in a village church on Salisbury Plain for the violin, flute, and violoncello, before the advent of the harmonium; and we know that in early days there were many such local uses.

Fig. 5 (*c*) shows another of the many attempts to combine the phonetic and the pictorial notations, and **Another Effort to combine the Phonetic and Pictorial Notations** there will be found in *Paléographic Musicale*, vol. ii., Plate 190, the photograph of part of the Montpellier Gradual of the eleventh century, in which alphabetical letters (from *a* to *k*) are written over the words, and above the letters are the neumes. This system, though without the neumes, is found in Plate 1 of *Early English Harmony*, published by the Plainsong and

---

[1] Burney, *History*, vol. ii. p. 38.

Early Efforts

Mediæval Music Society, said to date from the tenth century.

The year A.D. 1000 was, as is well known, supposed to be the one in which the world would end, and when men found that the seasons went on just as usual, that no break was made in the natural sequence of events,

FIG. 5.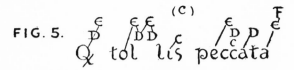

they took fresh heart, built cathedrals and churches, undertook Crusades, began to enjoy life, and generally to give evidence of the relief from the long suspense.

The new century saw the birth of our modern notation, and with this important epoch we begin a new chapter.

Translation of Fig. 5 (c):—

Qui - tol - - - lis pec - - ca - ta.

CHAPTER V.

GUIDO, or Guidone Aretino, or, in English, Guy of
Arezzo, to whom are attributed many important improvements in notation, was a Benedictine
monk who lived in the early part of the
eleventh century.   He was an ardent reformer, a man of great genius, and a good fighter in the
cause that he had at heart.   Naturally he made many
enemies, who, jealous and angry with him, succeeded
in getting him banished from his monastery, a proceeding which had the excellent effect of spreading his
teaching through Italy, and afterwards through Europe,
and now, after nine hundred years, we are still benefit-
ing by it.   *Beatus Guido, inventor Musicæ*, stands under
his portrait at Arezzo, so much did mediæval musicians
appreciate his genius.   His principal work was done at
the monastery of Pomposa, near Ravenna.   His chief
characteristic seems to have been practical common-

**Character
of Guido**

Guido's Sarcasms

sense, as opposed to the mystical dreamings of the ordinary writers, or the ignorant rule-of-thumb teaching of the ordinary singers.

The western world was at this time full of highly respected music-teachers from Italy, Greece, France, and Germany, but their ignorance (according to Guido) was astonishing; for example, he says, they could not distinguish between a note and its fifth: and their teaching was most unsatisfactory, though they had the highest possible opinion of themselves. Guido begins his "Rules for Unknown Song" (*i.e.*, Treatise on Sight-singing) with the following sarcasms:— " Of all living men, singers are the most fatuous (*Temporibus nostris super omnes homines fatui sunt cantores*); for in every art we know many things besides those which we have learned from our teacher. Little boys, if they have once arrived at sufficient knowledge to read through the Psalter, can read all other books; rustics can quickly understand the science of agriculture; he who has once pruned a vine, or once planted a tree, or once loaded an ass, will be able to do the same thing again, and probably better the second time: but these wonderful

Guido's opinion of Contemporary Singing Masters

NEUME NOTATION, PERIOD OF GUIDO.

Story of Notation

singing-masters, and their pupils, may sing every day for a hundred years, yet they will never be able to sing the smallest unknown antiphon without previous instruction ; so that they waste an amount of time with their wretched singing that would suffice for learning all the books in the world, both sacred and secular." He refers here, of course, to the use of the neumatic notation, which could not possibly show how to sing an unknown chant. "How can a man have the face to call himself a musician or singer, if he cannot sing at once, and correctly, a newly composed song?" His *Micrologus* contains the often-quoted sarcastic rhymes :—

> "*Musicorum et Cantorum*
> *Magna est distantia,*
> *Isti dicunt, illi sciunt*
> *Quæ componit Musica.*
> *Nam qui facit, quod non sapit*
> *Diffinitur bestia.*
> *Cæterum tonantis vocis*
> *Si laudent acumina*
> *Superabit philomela*
> *Vel vocalis asina,*" etc.

> "'Twixt a singer and musician
> Wide the distance and condition,
> One repeats, the other knows
> What doth harmony compose.
> He who works without a plan
> May be called more beast than man.
> If, of loud and thundering voice,
> Or shrill sounds, he makes a choice,
> Asses can bray louder still,
> Nightingales are far more shrill."

GUIDO OF AREZZO EXPLAINING HIS USE OF MONOCHORD TO
BISHOP THEODALDUS.

From *Gerbert's Scriptores.*

Guido and Notation

" It often sounds during the Mass, not as if we were singing the praise of God, but as if we were quarrelling amongst ourselves.

"The way of the philosophers is not my way; I concern myself only with what is useful to the Church, and can bring our youngsters on."

By these and similar sayings Guido did not fail to provoke hostility. Like all reformers, he had hosts of enemies, whose efforts to suppress him merely resulted in getting him more widely known. Let us now see what he did for musical notation.

Hostility against Guido

He tells us that he made his pupils become familiar with the lettering of the monochord. Gerbert, in his second volume, reproduces an ancient picture taken from a MS. at Vienna, representing "Guido Monachus" exhibiting his monochord to Bishop Theodaldus of Arezzo. He is plucking the string with the quill end of a feather, held in his left hand, while his right holds a kind of blunt knife, wherewith to stop the string at the points shown by the lettering, Gamma, A, B, C, D, E, F, G, *a, b, h, c, d, e, f, g,* on the body of the instrument. The designer of the picture evidently knew little about music, for his lettering would not produce anything like the proper intervals, and he omits the upper notes, designated by Guido, *aa, bb,* ♮♮, *cc, dd, ee.*[1] This lettering, which if

---

[1] These letters, called *excellentes,* were often placed one above the other—thus, a b c, / a b c, etc.

Story of Notation

not invented by Guido was confirmed by him, and has remained to the present day, embraces both the conjunct and disjunct tetrachords of the Greek system, and by Guido's time the note *trite synnemenon* was almost

Two Forms of b
universally indicated by the letter b, called *b rotundum,* or *b molle,* because it was round, and because it "softened" the harshness of the tritone f, b. The note *paramese* was given the sign ♮, called *b quadratum,* or *b durum;* the Germans call this note h, and in the picture it is given as h. Guido called the capital letters *graves* (low), the small letters *acutæ* (high), the double letters *super acutæ* (above the high). "Many blame these terms as superfluous, but we would rather have superfluity than deficiency."

"The soft *b* we mostly use in songs which start from F or *f;* G is the fourth note of the first authentic tone

Use of B flat
(the octave-species D-d) ; *a* is the fourth note of the second authentic tone (E to e); *b* of the third (F to f). If you wish to avoid the soft *b,* you must transpose the neumes in which it occurs, in such a way that you have the notes G, *a,* ♮, *c,* instead of F, G, *a, b.*" He also suggests that it is good practice to commence a melody on each of the four finals in turn, and sing it through with the semitones as given by the letters of the monochord. To make this plain by a modern example, it would be to sing "God save the King" first in the key of C, beginning on C, then in the same key, but beginning on D, then in the same key, but beginning on E, and again in the same key, but beginning on F. It must

The Hexachords

be remembered that at that time musicians, or at any rate church musicians, only knew the sounds represented by the monochord, *i.e.,* the white keys of our organ, together with *b rotundum;* the sharps and the four remaining flats were not yet invented. Hence, if the pitch was changed it could only be in the way suggested, or a fourth higher, with the use of *b rotundum.*

PRIEST PLAYING ON A HARP (EGYPTIAN).

The study of Greek music was imperative on every musician in those days; and the division of the scale into tetrachords probably suggested to Guido his division into hexachords. But it is a remarkable fact, showing the prophetic nature of his genius, that instead of using any of the church tones or the ancient Greek modes as the basis of his hexachords, he boldly struck

The Guido-nian Hexachords

out a new line, and used what is now known as the major mode, foreseeing that this must be the chief mode of the future. He was probably influenced by the secular musicians who were already using this

Story of Notation

mode; and we have seen that one at least of the inventors of notations endeavoured to adapt the Latin alphabet to it.

In addition to arranging a series of hexachords, he made use of a series of sounds for singing exercises, **Guido's** perhaps suggested by the τω, τα, τε, τη of the **Solmisation** singing exercises of Rome under the empire. (See page 40.) Each verse of a hymn to John the Baptist began on a note corresponding to the six notes of his principal hexachord. "Whoever," says he, "can, through practice, distinguish clearly the initial notes of each of these six lines, so that he can commence with any line taken at random, will be in a position to easily sing these six notes wherever he meets with them." The hymn in question was :—

C	*ut—quæant laxis*	F	*fa—muli tuorum*
D	*re—sonare fibris.*	G	*sol—ve polluti*
E	*mi—ra gestorum*	A	*la—bii reatum*

Sancte Johannes.

Doubt has been raised as to whether Guido was or was not the actual inventor of "solmisation," but the question cannot be discussed here. It is sufficient for our purpose that if Guido did not invent it, it came into use somewhere about his time. It was found that whether a hexachord began with G, C, or F, the same series of four tones, with one semitone, resulted. Hence each of these notes could become *ut* for singing purposes; and the system was analogous to that which many centuries afterwards was called the "movable *do.*"

78

Table of Hexachords

FIG. 6.

	Γ	A	B	C	D	E	F	G	a	b	c	d	e	f	g	aa	bb	cc	dd	ee
Monochord	Γ	A	B	C	D	E	F	G	a	b	c	d	e	f	g	aa	bb	cc	dd	ee
Guido	Ut	re	mi	fa	sol	la														
				Ut	re	mi	fa	sol	la											
							Ut	re	mi	fa	sol	la								
								Ut	re	mi	fa	sol	la							
											Ut	re	mi	fa	sol	la				
														Ut	re	mi	fa	sol	la	
															Ut	re	mi	fa	sol	la

The hexachords beginning on G were called *Hexachordum durum.* Those beginning on C were *Hexachordum naturale.* Those beginning on F were *Hexachordum molle.* In course of time these letters became the so-called "clefs."

Story of Notation

The syllable *ut* became afterwards changed to *do*, as being more easy to sing; and when harmony had succeeded to counterpoint, and the leading note had in consequence become prominent, the syllable *si* was added, about the end of the seventeenth century, to complete the seven notes of the major scale, which then became *Do, re, mi, fa, sol, la, si,* and the notes are thus named in France and Italy to this day.

The Modern Form of Solmisation

The cumbrous nomenclature used by Burney, Hawkins, and others was in force during the whole of mediæval times, and only disappeared at the end of the eighteenth century. This nomenclature, taken from the Guidonian hexachords, was as follows:—*Gam-ut,* A *re,* B *mi,* C *fa ut,* D *sol re,* E *la mi,* F *fa ut,* G *sol re ut, a la mi re,* etc., and every choir-boy was compelled to learn it by heart. Guido (or some one about his time) adapted this nomenclature to the joints of the fingers of the left hand, making his boys sing the notes as he pointed to the various parts of his hand. Starting from the top joint of the thumb, the scale worked down the thumb in a circle round the outside of the fingers, ending inside, but the highest note of all was given to the tip of the longest finger. The figure of the so-called "Guidonian Hand," on page 87, shows the order of naming of the joints in a more easily understood manner than in the old figures, where every joint is given its complicated hexachordal name: and the arrow-heads in the dotted line show the direction followed by the scale

The Guidonian Hand

Notation à Points Superposés

order. The Guidonian hand must have taken a great place in mediæval teaching, for it is described by nearly all writers on notation, and the "gamut" continued to be a useless worry to choir-boys for many centuries.

" Amongst the many temptations to inattention which surrounded the choristers in the seventeenth century was their right to claim money from any person entering the cathedral with spurs on his boots. This tax was called spur-money. It is said that the man challenged could call upon the chorister to repeat his *gamut:* if he failed to do so the tax was evaded, if he succeeded the money was paid." [1]

Spur-Money

We must now speak of the invention of the staff or stave, a thing so familiar to us and, from its familiarity, so apparently simple, that few people are aware of the immense number of experiments continued through many generations which were required to bring it to its present form. The first step towards it seems to have been the invention of a notation which the Benedictines have given the name of *Notation à Points Superposés*. Great care is taken by the scribe to make the points and the parts of the neumes show the intervals by their distance above the text, and above or below one another. This was probably done by laying parallel rulers on the parchment, and the natural result was that some one hit on the plan of drawing or

Rise of the Staff

Superposed Points

[1] Bevan and Stainer, *Handbook of St. Paul's Cathedral.*

81

Story of Notation

scratching a line across the page, as a guide to both the scribe and the reader. At the commencement **The Stave of One Line** of this line was placed a letter, generally F, and all points or portions of neumes which occurred on the line were meant to indicate the note F. The scale-degrees indicated by the rest of the neumes depended on the greater or less exactitude with which they were written above

FIG. 5.   (d)

and below the line. Fig. 5 (*d* and *e*) show a form of notation of which MSS. have been found in many parts of

FIG. 5.   (e)

Italy; having been invented at Nonantola, the Benedictines have called it the Nonantolian notation. It will be seen that vertical lines are drawn from each syllable

Clefs and Lines

to the horizontal line called F or a little above or below it. This line is not continuous, and is inked over a scratched line, without the aid of a ruler. A possible solution is given in modern notation.

The next step was the addition of another line, above F, which was intended to represent C ; this fixed two notes definitely, and facilitated the placing of the neumes representing sounds between C and F. The letters F and C, when applied to the lines in this manner, were called *Claves*, or in French, Clefs, that is keys, for, as Zarlino and others explain, they "unlock the door, and give access to the knowledge of the notes." Sometimes, though rarely, other letters, especially G, a, b, ♮, d, were used as claves. G, having been less used than C and F, has retained its shape better in the modern Treble Clef than the other two letters. (See Fig. 11, page 170.)

Stave of Two Lines

The preference for F and C is not far to seek. F was the beginning of a hexachord ; it was the lowest convenient note for reciting on ; and C was the beginning of another hexachord at a convenient distance from F ; and these two clefs were sufficient for plainsong. With the advent of measured music a third clavis, G, was added, so that the three claves represented the three kinds of hexachord, the *molle*, the *naturale*, and the *durum*.[1]

The choice of F and C as Clefs

[1] Ambros gives another reason. F and C are both represented by the syllable *fa*; and *mi fa*, the only semitone in the hexachord, is thus clearly shown by coloured lines.

83

Story of Notation

In course of time, a line was drawn half-way between F and c, which gave a; and now by placing G and b or ♮ between the lines, the sounds F, G, a, b, ♮, c, could be definitely fixed. Finally, a fourth line was added, either above C or below F, as was found convenient, and the stave of four lines, which has been used for plainsong to this day, was complete. For music other than plainsong extra lines were added above and below the original four, as we shall see in due course.

Stave of Three Lines

Stave of Four Lines

The lines were at first coloured, F being generally red, and C yellow; and when there was a third and fourth

NEUME NOTATION.

Coloured Lines

line, these were either scratched on the parchment by some pointed instrument, or drawn with black ink. There was no regular rule in the early days of lines. Thus the *Paléographie Musicale* gives two examples from Lombardy of the twelfth century, in which there is one line only, that is scratched, and no clef given, for it was supposed to represent no other note than F. In an eleventh or twelfth century MS. of Arezzo (the home of Guido), F is given as a red line, and there are two others scratched without clefs. Another three-line stave of the beginning of the twelfth century from Monte Cassino (a famous Benedictine monastery half-way between Rome and Naples) has F red, C yellow, the third scratched. A very usual combination for four lines was F red, C yellow, the remaining two scratched.

A so-lis or-tu us-que ad oc-ci-du-a Lit-to-ra

ma-ris planctus pulsat pec-to-ra; Ul-tra ma-ri-na

ag-mi-na tris-ti-ti-a Te-ti-git in-gens cum er-ro-re

ni-mi-o. Heu! me do-lens, plan-go!

TRANSLATION OF NEUME NOTATION. (From Crowest, *Story of British Music*, vol. i. p. 147.)

Story of Notation

This is found in a twelfth-century Gradual of St. Peter's at Rome, and in many other MSS. The red F was continued in some places till the fourteenth century—thus a Franciscan Breviary of that time in the Vallicellan Library at Rome has a three-line stave, red and two blacks, without clefs, while many MSS. of the thirteenth century have four black lines. In some cases, dating from the thirteenth century, we find four red lines used, as in the manuscript of "Sumer is icumen in"; and these are not uncommon to this day. By the fifteenth century the so-called Gregorian stave seems to have settled down entirely to four lines of the same colour, either black or red. But neumes continued to be written without lines for several generations after the invention of the stave. If it be asked why the stave should have taken so long to develop when we have seen that it was practically invented before the time of Guido, according to Galilei and Kircher, it may be answered that many inventions seem to die at their birth, only to re-appear in another form later. The staves shown on pp. 69, 70 seem to have been used only in a remote part of Sicily; they were probably unknown beyond its immediate locality, and even if known, their suitability for use with neumes would not be evident.

What part did Guido take in the invention of the stave, the most important feature of modern **Guido and the Stave** notation? The mediæval writers were so proud of him that they attributed its invention entirely to him, and called the new system

Guido and the Antiphonary

the Guidonian notation. Ambros tells us that the Magliabecchiana Library at Florence possesses a Missal of the tenth century, containing sometimes a red, sometimes a red and yellow line. If this date is correct, Guido did not invent the line notation, but there is no doubt whatever that he greatly improved it and confirmed its use.

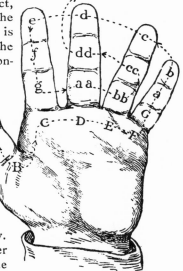

He, at any rate, added two new lines to the original two, and having thus produced a stave in which each degree of the scale had its own proper line or space, he applied it to the whole of the Antiphonary.

THE GUIDONIAN HAND.

He says that now, after many storms, calm came to him. He was forced to leave his monastery of Pomposa by the envy and malice his new inventions and his sarcasms had provoked; and Pope John XIX.,[1] hearing of the wonderful results of his teaching, invited him to Rome in company with an abbé, and Peter, the

[1] A.D. 1024-33.

Story of Notation

Provost of the Cathedral of Arezzo. The Pope made him explain the whole of his new system, repeatedly read the explanations given in his *De ignoto* **Guido is** *cantu,* which formed the prologue of the **invited to** Antiphonary, and did not rise from his seat **Rome** until he had sung correctly a versicle that was previously unknown to him. He looked upon the Antiphonary as a marvel of ingenuity, and wished to retain Guido in his service on the most favourable conditions. Guido's health, however, would not stand the Roman climate ; he became very ill of Roman

LYRE.

fever, as it was a hot summer, and was obliged to leave. But he promised the Pope to come again in the winter, and instruct the priests in the new method.

His work being recognised and appreciated by the Pope and the high officials at Rome, he returned to Pomposa and showed his Antiphonary to the abbot. **Received** The result was that the **favourably** abbot was now convinced **at his** that it was a good work, **Monastery** and expressed his sorrow that he had listened to Guido's enemies and forced him to leave the monastery. Guido was offered a bishopric, but he preferred to remain a "simple monk amongst monks, and to bring honour to his monastery by

A True Reformer

his work;" and it is probable that he ended his days at Pomposa.

Unlike the writer of *Enchiriadis* and his own contemporaries, Guido did not seek to bend the art of music to the obsolete rules of the Greek theorists, which were only applicable to a different, and, in its best days, far more highly developed form of art than his own. Taking music as he found it, he simply sought what was suitable for the time he lived in, and for getting the best results from the existing (not the past) conditions. This is what every reformer has done, and it is perhaps one of the strangest traits in the nature of man, that every one in every age and every country who works for the improvement of art, science, religion, knowledge, incurs jealousy, suspicion, and dislike; and, as Guido himself says, may be compared to the glassworker, who, having invented an unbreakable glass, is rewarded with death at the hands of the hangman.

CHAPTER VI.

Measured music—*Cantus figuralis, Discantus, Fauxbourdon*—*Contra-punctus*—The neumatic notation adapted to the needs of measured music—The rules given by Franco of Cologne—His five moods—The figures—Notes—The origin of the ternary time division, which was called perfect—Rules for the notes—Division of mood —Point or prick of perfection—The plica and ligatures—Propriety and perfection—Complications of the rules for ligatures—Disappearance of free rhythm—The original measurements of notes were not by ternary but by binary divisions—*Instans, tempus,* and *chronos protos*—Hieronymus of Moravia does not give measured values to notes—Johannes de Garlandia's rules—The *triplum.*

WE now come to the period at which modern European music may be said to begin.   We have seen that men

Beginning of Modern Music

had been making experiments with the "symphonies" of the Greek musicians, by singing in fourths and fifths and octaves. Further efforts were only natural, and fresh results were obtained by accident.   Thus it was found that the occasional use of diaphonies was not unpleasant; that thirds and sixths, though classed as discords by the Pythagoreans—for the Pythagorean teaching had now completely superseded that of Aristoxenus—could perfectly well be used as long as men trusted to the ear, and not to mathematics.   This had been observed many

Free Rhythm Disappears

centuries before by the Greek writer Gaudentius, but seems to have been forgotten until rediscovered and noticed by Franco of Cologne. But a further development took place. Instead of the old "note against note," a new form of art began, in which one or more singers sang several notes against each of the notes of the plain-song. The plainsong now lost all its rhythm, and was called *cantus planus, musica plana, cantus firmus, tenor,* while the accompanying voice or voices were called *musica mensurabilis* or *mensurata, cantus figuralis, cantus floridus, discantus,* Fauxbourdon, Faburden, contrapunctus;

PART OF A HYMN, NEUME NOTATION.

and the old writers divide Church music into "*cantus simplex planus,* which is in simple notes of uncertain value, whose mode is Gregorian"; "*cantus, Simplex figuratus,* that in which simple notes have a certain

Story of Notation

value"; "*cantus compositus,* in which many notes in one part are sung in due relation to the notes of the other"; "*cantus per medium,* in which two notes are measured against one of the plainsong."[1] To these must be added *Gymel,* or Gemellum, a kind of *twin song* used in England, for two voices, singing for the most part in thirds and sixths.

It soon became evident that it was impossible for singers to sing *cantus figuralis* unless there was some definite regulation of the number of notes to be sung against the sustained note of the *cantus firmus,* the fixed song; and hence arose a form of Notation called *musica mensurabilis,* or *mensurata—i.e.,* measured music; but not for centuries did musicians come to a complete understanding as to the details of the notation of the *cantus figuratus;* and in the end they were obliged to combine the *musica mensurata* of the learned Church musicians with the tablatures of the despised worldly instrumentalists, before they arrived at a satisfactory and easily understood notation. It is probable that many experiments were made in various places. The clearest information we have is that given by Franco of Cologne, who flourished at the beginning of the thirteenth century. He was preceded and followed by a number of writers on *musica mensurabilis,* who continued for the next three centuries working at the matter, and gradually evolving a satisfactory system.

Measured Music

Franco of Cologne

[1] Tinctor, *Proportionale,* in Coussemaker, vol. iv.

92

Measured Music

The idea of representing the intervals by means of the lines and spaces of the stave, to which was added one or more of the claves C, F, G, had taken root and spread over Europe, and it remained to invent a method of showing the relative time measurement of the notes which were placed on the stave. The virga had become the square-headed note ♩, and the punctum either a square ■ or a lozenge ◆; and these forms were taken as the basis of the new notation, in explanation of which we will allow some of these old writers to speak for themselves, beginning, not with the earliest, but with Franco, since he is the clearest. *"Musica mensurabilis* is song, measured by longs and shorts. I say *mensurabilis,* because in plainsong there is no measure. A 'Time' is a measure of sound or of silence, which is commonly called a rest.[1] I say that the rest is measured by time, because otherwise, two voice parts, of which one contains rests, while the other does not, could not be kept in their proper proportions." "Measured music is divided into wholly and partly measured. Wholly measured is discant, of which every portion is regulated by time. Partly measured is called organum, which is only occasionally measured." The organum was no longer strictly note against note.

"And you must know that the organum is used

Franco's Explanations

---

[1] We translate the Latin word *pausa* as "rest," since this is familiar to English musicians, who use "pause" for the Latin *fermata.*

93

Story of Notation

in two ways. The organum proper is the pure organum, but the general organum is when the plainsong is measured." Here we are reminded that, as
long as plainsong was only sung in unison
Plainsong or octaves, its notes were not measured, but
was not followed the natural pronunciation of the
Measured words. This fact has been too often lost
sight of by writers on plainsong, who have endeavoured
to give time-value to the neumes, and to the ordinary
notation of plainsong.

"Discant is the consonance of several different
melodies." Our author then proceeds to divide discant
into several kinds after the manner of all early writers
and some moderns, who seem unable to avoid classifying everything. The method of teaching counterpoint
still in vogue in England, and, we believe, in some
parts of the Continent, in which everything is classified
into five "species," is a direct outcome of mediæval
methods.

Franco now classifies time measurement into modes,
or moods.

"Some say there are six moods, some seven. We
reduce them to five."

I. — — — — All the notes long, or
— ◡ — ◡ — ◡ A long note followed by a short note.
II. ◡ — ◡ — ◡ — A short note followed by a long.
III. — ◡ ◡ — ◡ ◡ A long followed by two shorts.
IV. ◡ ◡ — ◡ ◡ — Two shorts followed by a long.
V. ◡ ◡ ◡ ◡ All shorts.

Perfection and Imperfection

"Concerning the Figures.

"Of figures, some are simple, others are compound. The compound figures are the ligatures. Of simple figures there are three kinds—the *longa*, the *brevis,* and the *semibrevis:* and the *longa* has three values—perfect, imperfect, and double.

"The long is called perfect when it is measured in three 'Times.'

"The Ternary is the most perfect of numbers, for it takes its name from the Trinity, which is pure perfection. The figure of the long is square, with a tail descending from its right side, ⏋

"The imperfect long is represented by the same figure. It contains two Times, and those are wrong who call it a *longa recta*.[1]

"An imperfect long can never stand by itself: it must always have a breve before or after it, and it is called imperfect for this reason." The confusion of theological doctrines with music was very great in these times: the number three must be preserved at all costs, therefore a two-time long must be completed by a breve to bring it to the ternary condition. It has been endeavoured to show in a recent historical work that the giving of ternary value to notes was not due to theological influence, but that the writers merely pointed out the similarity of "three notes in one" to the

---

[1] The original value of the long was two times, and the perfect or three-time long is of later invention. Hence perhaps the expression *longa recta* for two-time long.

doctrine of the Trinity. The argument taken is that
practical men would not acquiesce in an absurdity.
Though there is much to be said for this view, we
cannot agree with it; for the frequent discussions and
hairsplitting over mere words show that the Church
musicians were not practical. The practical men were

NOTATION OF SPANISH TROUBADOURS.

the despised "practitioners" of music—the lay instrumentalists, who had no connection with the Church,
and who never caused confusion by making triple
measure the basis of their notation.

"'The Double Long' has the form of two longs
which are joined together in one body, so that the
tenor of the plainsong may not be broken." That is
to say, the double long was used chiefly in the plain-

Longs and Shorts

song, which was the "tenor" or holding part, in order that the other singers might have plenty of time for florid ornamentation of their parts.

"The breve is either *recta* or otherwise. It is a square without a tail ■.

"The semibreve is either major or minor, and is formed like a lozenge ◆."

Elsewhere we learn that the *recta brevis* is divided into three semibreves, the "other" breve into two. The major semibreve is ternary, the minor binary.

"A long is followed by a long or a breve, and this is also the case with breves and semibreves. If a long follows a long, whether the second long is a rest or a note, the first will be measured by three Times, and is called a perfect long."

"But if a long is followed by one or more breves, it will be a two-time long, and is called imperfect; except when between the long and the breve there is placed a little upright line called a sign of perfection, or division of mood, in which case the first long is perfect, while the breve makes the long which follows it imperfect; thus—

Sign or Point of Perfection

Su - pe-rans om-ni-a,

which would be represented thus in modern notation—

Su - pe - rans om - ni - a.

97

Story of Notation

It will be seen then that the little upright line called the division of the mood is practically our bar line, though not till many centuries later was it used at regular intervals, as with us.

"But if two or three or four or more breves follow the long, then the long is perfect; unless it is *preceded* by a single breve." The whole difficulty arises from there being as yet no means of showing the regular measures, for the full significance of the *divisio modi* was not yet understood.

"Of two breves, the first is *recta* (ternary), the second binary. The *brevis recta* contains one whole time: the *brevis altera* is analogous to the imperfect long in value, for both, though represented by different figures, are measured by two times, but what is called a single time of the breve is the minimum time that the voice is capable of uttering distinctly." Here we have the origin of our word "minim"; and when it became necessary to use notes of less value than the *minima,* the theorists objected that one could not have anything less than the least. "But if between two longs there occur two breves, and between the two breves there is a division of mood, then the two longs are imperfect, and of the two breves, either you like will be *recta;* but this very rarely occurs." Franco gives the following example:—

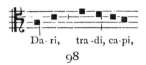

Da· ri,   tra -di, ca·pi,

Point of Perfection

equivalent to

Da - ri,   tra - di,   ca - pi,

in which there seems no object in considering the breves as of three or two-time value in themselves; for they are simply the complement of the imperfect longs. "But if three breves occur between two longs they will each be *recta,* unless influenced by the division of mood between the first two of the three breves, in which case the first long is imperfect, the middle breve is *recta.* And whatever contains three times, whether uttered with one accent or more, constitutes perfection." We now come to the origin of our "dotted note."

"If several breves follow a long, the long is always imperfect unless the sign of perfection is added to it." The sign of perfection with Franco is a little bar, similar to the division of mood; it afterwards became the "Point of Perfection," or in England the "Prick of Perfection," namely, our dot after a note. **The Dotted Note**

"Of the breves which follow, any must be made *recta* that may be necessary in order to produce the ternary number, which constitutes perfection." That is to say, three time must be adhered to throughout.

"But if at the end of a group of breves there are two

99

Story of Notation

remaining, then the last must be considered as *altera brevis*, thus:—

Literally:—

but natural instinct would probably lead the singer thus:—

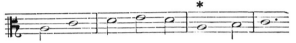

for which apparently the long followed by a breve would not do, because the singer would consider it as affected by the previous breve, and syncopate it, as in the first bar. The rules the unfortunate singer was obliged to learn were terribly complex, owing to the want of a simple expedient of indicating the measures with exactness.

"But if there is only one breve left, it will make the last long imperfect."

"Now concerning semibreves, the rules are the same as for breves; but more than three semibreves cannot be contained in a *brevis recta*. Of these three semibreves each is called minor; it is the least part of a *recta brevis*. And if the breve contains two semibreves, the first is called minor, the second major, for it contains two minors."

Influence of Neumes

The accentuation of the minor and major semi-breves depended on their position with regard to the longer note that preceded or followed them. It is unnecessary to quote the rules for semi-breves, as they arrive at the same result as those for breves, everything being arranged so as to produce triple measure. **Accentuation**

In the sixth chapter Franco treats of the Plica (Fig. 7, p. 105), which is the *epiphonus* and *cephalicus* of the neumes.[1] He and his contemporaries had not arrived at the idea that a syllable which begins on a high and ends on a low sound, or *vice versâ*, is sung to two or more *notes;* under the influence of the neumatic notation, they considered that the sound was all one, that it began low and ended high, or that it moved up and down, and must therefore be represented by one figure, or, as they said, by one note. Hence arose all the troublesome complications of the ligatures, the proper translation of which is exceedingly puzzling. Franco begins his chapter on this subject thus :—

"The plica is a note in which the same sound is divided into high and low." "The plica may be a long, a breve, or a semibreve"—*i.e.*, it is not two short notes, but one single note proceeding upwards or downwards. **The Plica**

"The semibreve plica cannot occur in simple figures, but it is possible in ligatures, as will appear later. Plicas are ascending or descending. The long plica is a square figure having an ascending line on its right,

[1] See p. 60.

Story of Notation

with a shorter one on its left; and from these two lines comes its name plica "—folded together. (See Fig. 7, p. 105.)

"The descending long plica has two lines, the right being longer than the left. In the ascending short plica the left-hand line is the longer, and in the descending short, the left is also the longer. And note that the plicas have the same powers and values as the simple notes described above."

We now come to the Ligatures (Fig. 7), which arose directly from the *porrectus*, the *torculus*, the *climacus*, and *salicus* of the neumes, as shown **Ligatures** in Fig. 3, p. 55. The reader will remember that a thick oblique line in a ligature merely represents two notes, which, as Morley says,[1] stand at the beginning and the end of the line.

Let us now see what Franco has to say about ligatures; and we must observe that from here he uses the word *punctus,* "point," to indicate what we should call the notes, for *nota* and *figura* mean the complete ligature —i.e., a continuous sound running over two or more degrees of the scale.

"An ascending ligature is one in which the second point is higher than the first." Here we meet with one of the most complicated and strange parts of the teaching, so involved that it is a marvel that any one could sing at sight in those days.

"Ligatures are either with propriety, without pro-

[1] *Plain and Easy Introduction to Practical Music,* 1597. Page 10 of reprint, 1771.

102

Propriety and Ligatures

priety, or with opposed propriety. And this is with regard to the beginning of the ligature, for the latter part is either with perfection or without: and note that these differences are essential to the ligatures; for a ligature with propriety differs from one that is without, as a rational animal differs from an irrational one."

"Propriety is the chief note in the construction of the ligature, and occurs in its beginning: while perfection is the chief note at its end." Elsewhere we read, "Every propriety is short, impropriety long; opposed propriety produces two semibreves, since one alone is not used in a ligature, nor are more than two. Whence, if several notes come into a ligature, they are as follows: each perfect note is long, each imperfect note is a breve except those that are made semibreves by opposed propriety."

The meaning of the foregoing sentences becomes clear by further quotations.

"Every descending ligature having a line descending from its left side is said to be with propriety"—*i.e.*, its first note is short (see Fig. 7, p. 105). "But if it has no line at all it is without propriety"—*i.e.*, its first note is long.

"Every ascending figure is with propriety if it has no stroke at all."

"But if it has a stroke on the left or right of the first note, it is without propriety"—*i.e.*, the first note of an ascending ligature is short if there is no tail, long if it has a tail on its left side.

"Every ligature, whether ascending or descending,

103

Story of Notation

which bears a line rising from its first point, is with opposed propriety "—that is, its two first notes are semibreves. " But there is no essential difference in the middle of the ligature, all the notes of which are short."

The rules for the final note of the ligature now follow, and for the sake of brevity they may be epitomised: when the last note is long, the ligature is said to be " with perfection "; when short, it is " without perfection." The last note is long if it stands immediately over its predecessor, or if it stands under it and separated from it. It is short if it stands obliquely over or under its predecessor, and joined to it. With a rising or falling line joined to the right-hand side of the last note of the ligature, it is said to be " plicated," and if, being plicated, the last note is not joined to its predecessor, it is a long; if plicated and joined, it is a breve.

Guilielmus, the monk, gives a table of ligatures (Coussemaker, *Scriptores,* vol. iii. p. 276) marked with the letters L for long, b for breve, m for maxima, s for semibrevis, which, allowing for probable slips of the pen, agrees fairly well with the above rules.

Rests (Fig. 7) have now to be considered. A perfect long rest, of the value of three times, is an upright line covering three spaces. An imperfect long **Rests** rest covers two spaces. A breve rest, containing only one time, covers one space. A major semibreve rest covers the upper half of a space. The minor semibreve rest (minima) covers the lower half of

Plica, Ligatures, and Rests

FIG. 7.
Plica.

Ascending | ♩ Long / ♭ Short   Descending | ♩ Long / ♩ Short

Descending Ligatures.

With Propriety   Without Propriety   With Opposed Propriety

Ascending Ligatures.

Rests.

Perfect Long. Imperfect. Breve. Major Semib. Minor. End of Song.

Semiminima. Croma. Semicroma. End of Period

Story of Notation

a space. The end of the period is indicated by an unmeasured rest, extending above and below the stave.

"And note," says Franco, "that rests have a marvellous power; for by them the moods are interchanged among themselves."

Thus far Franco. We have quoted from him first, because he is clearer than others; the whole matter had probably become fairly settled by his **Changes of** time. We will now see what his pre-**Tempo** decessors have to say. The author of **were used** *Enchiriadis*, Hucbald or Odo, in whose **before** day measured music had not yet arisen, **Measured** nor the necessity for it, is quite alive to the **Music was** importance of slow and rapid tempo: for he **invented** remarks that not only the pitch but also the rapidity of the song must be varied according to the season; but that the singers must always attend to the enunciation of the neumes, which must be sung at a suitable pace, and neither with tedious slowness, nor with such irreverent haste as to sound like the bark of a dog. But at this time the rhythm, which consisted of groups of syllables and of neumes, was unmeasured: it was like the prose rhythm of the Psalms and other poetry in the Bible.

Riemann supposes that the old free rhythm began to give way to the measured music described by Franco in the eleventh and twelfth centuries, and that the "moods" formed the starting-point of the new teaching. The oldest writers on measured music are

Early Theory of Time

Hieronymus de Moravia, "Anonymus No. 7" of Coussemaker, and Johannes de Garlandia, an English musician who lived and taught at Paris. These inform us that in the earliest times the long was equal to two breves, not three; and it is unfortunate that they mixed music with theology and thus produced inextricable confusion. *The earliest Writers on Mensural Music*

Hieronymus de Moravia calls the smallest and indivisible tone which can be heard clearly and distinctly *instans,* "an instant," and says that this is what the ancients called a *Tempus,* a Time. Here we have a distinct outcome of Greek theory; for Aristoxenus builds the whole system of Greek musical rhythm on combinations of the *chronos protos—i.e.,* primary time, which, he says, is the shortest time value in a given composition, and is indivisible. "Some notes," Hieronymus says, "are long, some short, some very long, others very short." He gives the forms of the long, the breve, and the semibreve, as Franco does, and then describes a *nota longior, nota longissima, nota brevior, nota brevissima.* The first note of any chant is long, and if any syllable has more than one note, the second note is long. He then describes the plica and ligatures, and among rests he describes the *suspirium,* "an apparent rest which only exists for one instant." We should say a breathing place. It is striking how much place the single "Time" took in early theory. Under the heading "Discantus" we *The earliest ideas of Time Division seem to have been based on Greek teaching*

Story of Notation

have "measurable music is that which is measured by the measure of one or many 'Times.'" *Ultra mensuram* is said of notes which are of less value than one, or of more value than two "times," such as a succession of three semibreves; and it must be observed that every note of plainsong is long and *ultra mensuram*, since it contains the measure of three "times," that is to say when it is joined to discant: for it was still unmeasured if sung alone.

Johannes de Garlandia mentions six moods, dividing that described by Franco (page 94) as No. 1 into two, and **The Six Moods of Johannes de Garlandia** giving different numbers from Franco. He says that other teachers add other moods. He speaks of a *recta brevis* as containing one time, a *recta longa* as containing two *rectæ breves*, an oblique long, which is greater than a *recta longa*, a double long, which contains several longs in itself, and a long which turns itself towards higher and lower sounds—*i.e.*, a ligature, or, in modern parlance, a *legato* passage. He divides the moods into perfect and imperfect, describes the ligatures, with propriety, without propriety, and with opposed propriety, with and without perfection; the plicated ligatures, etc. The chapter on Ligatures is with all these writers long and obscure: if only they could have foreseen the simple modern use of the legato sign, how much trouble they would have saved themselves and us!

The Rest, he tells us, is a division of the sound, made in due proportion. Rests are simple and compound.

Johannes de Garlandia

Simple rests are those which cause a cessation of sound according to the value of some mood or manner, and they may be perfect or imperfect. The perfect rest does not change the mood, but **Rests** the imperfect changes it (from trochaic to iambic, etc.). A compound rest is double or triple or quadruple, etc. We should say that there were rests during two or three or four bars, etc. He gives the same forms for rests as Franco (page 104).

The division of the moods is a little perpendicular stroke placed below any line ; it is sup- **Division of** posed to be shorter than the rest for the **Mood** *recta brevis*.

Division of the syllables is the same—it occurs also in many plainsong MSS. in square notation **Division of** to show the musical, not the verbal syllables, **Syllable** for groups of notes were called syllables. A *suspiratio* he describes as an "apparent and non-existent rest, shorter than a *recta brevis.*"

Having explained the notation, he shows how it is used for discant. The tenor is, he says, called the first part, the discant the second part. The **Discant** first part has to be considered in three ways: as to melody, as to the number of points[1] it contains, and as to the mood or disposition of long and short notes. As to the second part, the discant, we have to consider in three ways also: as to the number of notes, which, though differing in quantity, must be together of equal value to those in the tenor ; as to mood,

[1] *I.e.*, single notes.

Story of Notation

which must agree with that of the tenor; and as to concordance, that the two parts sound well together. And to obtain "colour" when two points are taken with one of the tenor, either may be a discord. All authors allow this licence, which often occurs in the organum, and especially in motets. The *Triplum*[1] is a third part added to the discant. He describes the *recta longa* as a square with a tail, the *dupla* or *superabundans longa* as double the length of the first, and the plica, which differs in several respects from the plica of Franco.

KITHARA. *a*, ITS PLECTRUM.

We occasionally read of the sums paid to priests who could "organise" and sing in triplum and quadruplum. Du Cange quotes a passage from the Necrologium, or burial register of Paris of the thirteenth century, an order for the clerks who shall sing the *Alleluia* in organum, triplum, or quadruplum, to receive sixpence; and another passage orders that the four *organisers* of the Alleluia receive twopence each.[2]

[1] *Anglice*, treble, tribble, quatrible.
[2] Burney, vol. ii. p. 136.

CHAPTER VII.

Extracts from the writings of various fourteenth-century authors on measured music—"Sumer is icumen in"—Probably few such "rondels or common songs" were written down—Gymel—Magister de Garlandia — Odington — False music — Tendency of mediæval music to modulate to the subdominant due to retention of the Greek *synnemenon* tetrachord in the system—The raising of the leading note by false music produced the modern tendency of modulation to the dominant—Robert de Handlo's dialogue—Hamboys —A complicated time-table—De Muris of Paris and De Muris the Norman—Incompetent singers—Comparison of the old and new methods — Various time-signatures — Ecclesiastical objections to complicated music.

SUCH was the teaching, with slight variations, from about the middle of the twelfth century; and the ligatures held their place, though becoming more and more rare, until the eighteenth century. They are described in English by Morley, 1597, in Spanish by Cerone di Bergamo, 1613, are found in Trabercus's *Passion Music,* printed in Naples in 1635, and even in the examples of Martini's book on Counterpoint, printed at Bologna as late as 1774.

Coussemaker prints no less than forty tracts on measured music belonging to the fourteenth century alone ; and it is evident that if forty have survived the continental wars, accidental fires, and other forms

Story of Notation

of destruction, a very great number must have been written; and we know that the composers, especially **Numbers of Musical Treatises must have been produced** Englishmen, were numerous and held in great esteem at this time. There is an old and exploded tradition that counterpoint began in England. There is this much foundation for it that part singing was strenuously cultivated in England, and, at a very early epoch, reached a high degree of perfection. The famous canon, "Sumer is icumen in," composed by **"Sumer is icumen in"** John of Reading in 1250, cannot be a single effort; it must have been preceded by hundreds of similar compositions, or it could not have reached so high a standard of development. It is one of the "rondels and common songs" referred to by Johannes of Garlandia, who, speaking of the "colour" produced by "florification" of the notes, says, "Repetition of the same note is a colour by which the hearing is pleased; and we use this kind **The Common Songs were probably not often written down** of ornament in rondels and common songs." Students of modern counterpoint will recall the prohibition of repetition of a note, an outcome of mediæval teaching. It is probable that few of the rondels were written down. The priests, who were busy inventing a notation on theological lines, would not be very eager to make use of it for what they regarded as worldly music, and as such, opposed to the Church; and the common musicians, the Troubadours, Minnesingers, Meistersingers, etc., mostly sang their

Magister de Garlandia

songs by heart, and appear to have extemporised, in England, at all events, a kind of part-singing in thirds called *Gymel,* and in thirds and sixths called *Fauxbourdon.* Riemann derives the curious word Gymel from Gemellum—twin-song.

A second Magister de Garlandia, who lived a century later than Johannes, uses the word "propriety" with regard to the position of the song on the gamut. "There are in every song three proprieties, ♮ or *b* square, *b molle,* and natural. We know the ♮ because it begins on Γ, or *gamma-ut,* and ends with E, or it begins with G *sol re ut* and ends with e. *B molle* we know because it begins with F and ends with d. The natural propriety we know because it begins with C."

The Three Pitches at which a song could be sung

"In plainsong four lines are drawn because there are only seven notes; but in *cantus mensurabilis* five lines are drawn because nine notes are required for the *cantus organicus* in motets and elsewhere." Although plainsong uses now, and from the time of Guido has used, four lines, the added parts have used three, four, five, six, or any number that the composer has thought fit.

The Four and Five Lined Staves

Walter Odington, monk of Evesham, wrongly described as Archbishop of Canterbury, flourished in 1275. His treatise called *De Speculatione Musicæ* is mostly mathematical, and he gives the ancient Greek notation. He describes

Walter Odington

the claves, our clefs, as signs which inform us of the names of the notes, for without them we should not know the notes. He seems to be the first to divide the semibreve into three parts, the new note being called *Minima*.

The first Garlandia and an anonymous writer calling himself Aristotle, whom Coussemaker places as about contemporary with Franco of Cologne, are **False Music** among the first who speak of *Musica falsa*. Aristotle says, "Now the question arises, What necessity is there to make rules about false music or false mutation? For what is false ought not to be regulated, but what is true: false music and false mutation are, however, not without their use, but are, on the contrary, necessary to produce good consonances.

"We say that music becomes false when we change a tone to a semitone, or a semitone to a tone. It is not, however, really false, but changed, and it is done by placing the sign ♮ *quadratum*, or *b rotundum*, in the place that is to be changed."

But Garlandia is more explicit: "False music, which is very necessary for instruments, especially for the organ, occurs when we use a semitone for a tone and the reverse. Every tone may be divided into two semitones, therefore the number of signs which indicate the semitone may be increased in all the modes."

Walter Odington says, "The two b's belong to the monochord; the other alterations are called by musicians *falsa musica*, not because they contain any-

False Music

thing dissonant, but because they are outside the disposition of the monochord, and were not used by the ancients."

Here we have the origin of the term false music, afterwards called *musica ficta,* feigned music, and *musica inusitata,* unusual music. It arose simply from the fact that the monochord, the instrument used in teaching, and in proving the correctness of singing, contained no means of producing the semitones between the sounds called A, B, C, etc. Therefore any sound occurring between these degrees of the monochord was called a false sound, for it answered to no true note of the monochord. *B rotundum* was not a false sound, for it always had a place on the monochord, as had *b quadratum,* both of these notes belonging to the Greek systems. Some of the early writers dislike the use of a thing that is false; hence perhaps the change of name to *ficta.* The first false note that was used was occasioned by the transposition from the key of F to the key of B♭, necessitating a new note below E which was called E *b mollis* (in French now called E *bémol*). This transposition to the subdominant rather than to other degrees was suggested by the trite *synnēmenōn,* the *B rotundum;* for as we have shown in Chapter II., the Greek trope contained within itself the suggestion of this transposition, its synnemenon tetrachord being identical with the middle tetrachord of the key a fourth above it.

Introduction of E Flat into the Scale

In modern music the most natural modulation is to

Story of Notation

the dominant, a fifth above the key; for instead of destroying our leading note, we introduce a new one, the upper tetrachord of the first key **Modulation** becoming the lower of the new key.
to the
Dominant The tendency to modulate to the subdominant before the dominant is noticeable throughout the compositions of the fifteenth and sixteenth centuries. The predominance of the leading note in harmony during the early seventeenth century caused the change to the modern tendency towards the dominant. Perhaps an example will make this clearer. Example of transposition of the scale of C major on the monochord.

The tetrachord A becomes the upper half of the transposed scale; the *b rotundum* of the monochord practically enforces transposition to the subdominant, and suggests modulation thereto.

Modern use—

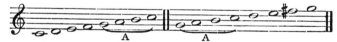

Here the tetrachord A becomes the lower half of the new scale; and the "false music," F sharp, which was not contained on the monochord, allows of upward instead of downward transposition and modulation.

Rules of False Music

After the *b rotundum* had been used for the note E, the *b quadratum* was used to contradict it; and when a false note was required between C and D, F and G, etc., the *b quadratum* was used for this purpose, and called *diesis*. It afterwards became a double cross (see Fig. 8, p. 118), called *crux,* and finally took the shape familiar to us. **The Natural and Sharp** The modern German name for sharp is *Kreuz,* meaning a cross, while the French call it *dièse.* Both nations also preserve the ancient expression *quadratum*—in French, *becarré,* square, German, *quadrat* for our "natural."

False music was not usually written for some centuries, because it was not on the monochord; and the singers had to learn by rule how to introduce it. The rules were fairly simple. At first it was used to correct an augmented fourth or diminished fifth; later, as harmony developed, it was introduced to form a perfect or complete *clausula,* **False Music was not written at first** our *close,* the note below the keynote being raised a semitone if necessary; or, in the mediæval expression, it introduced the interval *mi fa* into the perfect close if it was not there already. But supposing for any reason, by an exception to the rule, an F or C or any other note were *not* to be sung sharp, a flat was **Written Flats and Sharps not to be sung** written before or over them; while if B or E or other note were *not* to be flattened in the singing, a sharp was placed before them. An unwritten

Story of Notation

sharp or flat was to be sung; a written one did not
alter the note. These rules hold good for continental

FIG. 8.

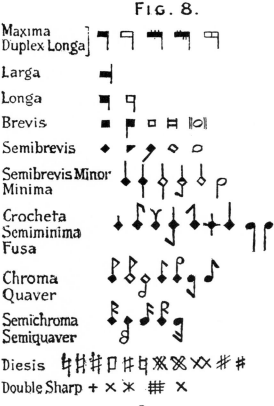

Maxima
Duplex Longa

Larga

Longa

Brevis

Semibrevis

Semibrevis Minor
Minima

Crocheta
Semiminima
Fusa

Chroma
Quaver

Semichroma
Semiquaver

Diesis

Double Sharp

118

The Sharp

music. English composers have always been more careful than their continental contemporaries to indicate the so-called "accidentals," and the first five forms of the diesis (Fig. 8) are copied from a fourteenth-century English MS., which abounds in accidentals. They were placed indifferently before, above, or below the notes they affected.

A curious little chapter added at the end of one of the anonymous treatises speaks about the sharp under the title *De Sinemenis,* a hybrid word, evidently taken from the Greek *synnēmenōn,* conjunct, and referring to the sharp as a conjunction between the tones. The writer speaks of the *crux*, cross, occurring between *b rotundum* and c, but in this case it is represented by the sign ♮. The *crux* also occurs between F and G, C and D, G and A, A and B, D and E. Here we have a complete chromatic scale. "And according to the vulgar, such music is called false music."

An anonymous chapter on the Sharp

In an imaginary dialogue dated 1326, between Robert de Handlo, an Englishman, and Franco of Cologne, a rising tail is placed on the right hand side of the *longa,* and the left of the *brevis,* when they represent semitones from the previous note, thus—

Tailed Notes representing Semitones

> *Erecta Longa* ♩,
> *Erecta Brevis* ♭,

which must have caused confusion.

Story of Notation

The same treatise shows a "plicated" semibreve when three semibreves are used with one syllable. This is also given by Petrus de Cruce and other writers. Its form is this: ◆ ◆ ♩. A new term occurs

Semilonga in De Handlo's treatise, the *semilonga*, whose figure, however, is the same as that of the long. The *duplex longa* is of the value

Duplex longa of six times if standing alone, but of five times if preceded or followed by a breve.

Handlo gives Franco's rules in the form of a dialogue between himself and Franco and others, and adds rules of his own, and of his contemporaries. He

Minoratæ Semi-breves speaks of *minoratæ semibreves,* diminished semibreves, which are formed like minimas, that is, with a tail ♩. In this treatise we find, as we should expect, all the complicated rules about ligatures.

The next author in Coussemaker's collection is another Englishman, Johannes Hanboys or Hambois

Dr. Hambois or Hamboys, whom Holinshed describes as "an excellent musician, and for his notable cunning therein made Doctor of Music." He complains that Franco has not given enough

The Crotchet explanations. He invents two new notes, the *crocheta,* like a *minima,* but having a shorter tail, and the *larga,* like a duplex longa, but having two tails (see Fig. 8, p. 118).

The Larga The larga contained nine longas if standing by itself, but ·longas standing before or after it were subtracted from its value. Thus,

De Muris the Norman

says Hamboys, if a larga is perfect, it contains 3 double longs, 9 longs, 27 breves, 81 semibreves, 243 minor semibreves, 729 semiminors, 2,187 minimas. What a complicated time-table for choir-boys to learn! **A Complicated Time-table**

There seem to have been two writers of the name of De Muris; one, called Johannes or Julianus, was made Rector of Paris University in 1350, and the other, Johannes de Muris, called the Norman, seems to have studied in Paris, but lived and taught at Oxford. **De Muris**

Johannes the Norman wrote a work called *Speculum Musicæ* in 1321, treating, amongst other things, of the whole system of Greek music with its notation, and of the notation of his own time, and here his treatise is of great value. He mentions a kind of notation in which a stave of four lines is drawn over the words, and instead of notes alphabetical letters are placed on the lines and spaces. He says that this is preferable to the old Greek notation which he has just described, but that it has the disadvantage of not showing the time value of the alphabetical letters, therefore it can only be used for plainsong. For mensurable music he says the square notation is necessary, and proceeds to describe it, saying that Guido invented it, which, however, he did not, for Guido knew nothing of measured music. Johannes devotes Chapter IX. of his seventh book to an interesting description of the incompetent singers of his day. We **Combination of Letter Notation with Stave**

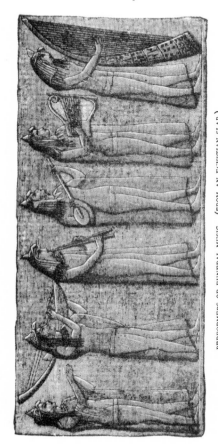

PERFORMERS OF FUNERAL MUSIC. (FROM AN EGYPTIAN SLAB.)

have seen that Guido had much to say on this matter; and it is an ever-recurring subject of complaint. "There are singers," De Muris says, "who have the impudence to sing, and to compose discant, when they know absolutely nothing of the nature of consonances; who cannot distinguish between major and minor concords, who are ignorant of many other things necessary to know, who sing a discant in such a manner above the tenor, that if by chance they succeed in making it

Mediæval Singers

Complaints against Innovations

concordant, it is no more than if a stone thrown by chance should hit a mark. . . . They mutilate, curtail, and corrupt the song; and if by good luck they light on a concord, such is their ignorance that they at once proceed to a discord. Alas! What grief! And some endeavour to cover their defects by saying that the new method of discant uses new consonances. They offend the intelligence and the senses of all who know their faults; for when they ought to give delight they produce only dejection. Oh, what evil plausibility, what irrational excuses, what great abuse, what ignorance, what bestiality! It is as if an ass were considered a man, a goat taken for a lion, a sheep for a fish, a snake for a salmon. . . . Oh, if our ancient learned doctors of music could hear such singers, what would they have said, what would they have done? . . . There are some who know how to sing in the modes yet do not observe them; others who discant lasciviously, and superfluously multiply the notes; some of these hoket[1] too much, break their notes[2] too much in the consonances, leap, and divide the discant at inopportune places, howl, shriek, and bark like a dog, feed on vexations, use far-fetched harmony."

"There are also in these times many good and worthy musicians, singers and discanters, who, being learned in the art, compose many beautiful discants, but they use the new method of singing and lay aside the old;

[1] Hoketus, a kind of discant, in which many rests occur.
[2] *Frangere voces* means to break the long notes into ornamental flourishes: hence *musica fracta*, broken music.

Story of Notation

they make too much use of imperfect semibreves, which they call minims, and instead of the old organised songs, the *conductus*, the motets, the double, contra, double and triple hokets, they insert in their motets things that are subtle and difficult to sing." It is evident that De Muris was *laudator temporis acti*, and was much troubled, like many a one before and after him, by the innovations which were being brought into the growing art of discant.

The Singers not all incompetent

He objects to the division of the semibreve. "The ancients say it is indivisible, while the moderns say it is not, and they call its divisions minimas." Concerning the figure of the semibreve, he says there is great dissension: "some cut it in half, others half fill it, others place a tail above or below it, others make it like a dragma.[1] Those who use semiminims or semiminores bend the tail to the right;" and he gives a most confusing list of the various names used by different writers to indicate the same things, showing that the notation was far from being settled as yet.

Confusion in Teaching

He devotes a long chapter to the discussion of whether the plicated semibreve should have its tail attached to the obtuse or the acute angle, and he objects to "the moderns," who use single semibreves, which is repugnant to nature; for *semi* is half, and it requires two halves to make a whole. He, like many a modern musician, compares the old simple music with the more

[1] See Fig. 8, p. 118. The Dragma is a lozenge with four tails.

Mediæval Time Signatures

difficult and subtle music of his day to the disadvantage of the latter; and his writings show that music was advancing. "Some moderns," he says, "consider those who do not cultivate the new art to be uncultured, uneducated, unlearned, and ignorant; and they look upon the old art as barbarous, irrational, but the new as exquisite and rational. Ought that to be called exquisite in which the effect of good concordance is lost, the measure is confounded, the words are not heard?

"The old mensurable art was slight and clear compared with modern. For the moderns use many rules for their longs and breves and semibreves: and because there are many moods in their De Muris's singing, some of them place a round circle views on to show perfect time, because the circle is a the Old perfect form. Thus— and New

Styles

"But others place three upright strokes to show perfect time. Thus—

"And these strokes must cover lines and part of the spaces to distinguish them from those which represent rests. And he who uses this teaching exclaims loudly against those who do not, calling them ignorant and uncultured.

"And to show Perfect Mood they use three lines enclosed in a quadrangle (see Fig. 9, p. 126).

"And for Imperfect Mood two lines in a quadrangle (Fig. 9).

125

Story of Notation

" But others use two half-circles for Imperfect Mood (Fig. 9).

FIG. 9.
Time Signatures.

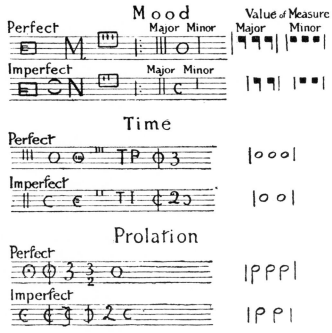

" And by such signs they denote Time and Mood, and they cannot denote one without the other.

Mediæval Time Signatures

"Some again presume to use M for Perfect Mood, and N for Imperfect, saying that as O. and C are used for variations of Time, so M and N may show Mood. But others reverse the matter and use O for Perfect Mood and Perfect Measure, C for Imperfect Mood and Imperfect Measure. Others use for Perfect Time a circle containing three strokes, thus, ⊚, and for Imperfect Mood a semicircle containing two strokes, ℂ (Fig. 9). Such, and many other things, do the moderns, which the ancients never did; and thus they have added many burdens to the art, which was formerly free, but which now has become like a slave in such matters." Here he ends: and his recriminations are important, since they describe early forms of what we should now call the Time Signatures.

Mood, of course, referred to the division of longs and shorts, according to the five or six moods; or, as we should say, mood **Mood** contained one long or its value in a bar.

Time referred in the same way to the semibreve, which, as we have seen, was a "Single Time" in the sense of the Primary Time of the Greeks. **Time** The signature for Time indicated a measure of one breve, and later it came to indicate a measure of one semibreve in value, which it still has.

To Mood and Time was afterwards added Prolation, which will be described in a later chapter.

The new notation and music were objected to by the Church. A bull was issued at Avignon about 1322

127

to suppress the innovations under severe penalties. "Some disciples of the new school," it was said, "while they apply themselves to measured times,

Objections to the New Art introduce new notes, prefer their own to the ancient chant; the Church music is sung in semibreves and minims, and is killed with little notes. They intersect the melodies with hoquets, slide about in discant, and sometimes even load and crowd the chants with *tripla* and common motets."

PERFORMERS ON LYRES (GREEK).

But John of Salisbury, a century and a half previously, had complained that the rites of religion were profaned by music, and that the stupid crowd, delighted with all these vagaries, imagined that they heard a concert of Sirens, in which the performers strive to imitate the notes of nightingales and parrots, not those of men.[1]

[1] Burney, vol. ii. p. 149.

Scandalous Singing

The times were barbarous, and there is no doubt that while the more earnest musicians were striving to improve the new art, many of the singers were doing their best to bring obloquy upon it by their scandalous singing.

CHAPTER VIII.

MARCHETTUS of Padua distinguishes between music and mathematics thus: "If it is asked what is the most

Marchettus of Padua
perfect in numbers, two or three, we should say two; but if it is asked which is the most perfect in music, two or three, we should

say three, for three contains two." He distinguishes

Discrepancies between French and Italian Schools
between French and Italian teaching—*e.g.*, if of two notes one is tailed, then, according to the Italians the tailed note, whether it is the first or the second, contains three times, the untailed only one; thus ♀ ◊ is equivalent not to ⌐⌐ but ⌐·⌐ Accord-

Red Notes

ing to the French, the tailed note is not divided by
quaternary division as above, but contains five parts
out of six, and is equivalent to ♪ ♪ ♪ ; and several pages
follow showing similar differences between Gallic and
Italian teaching.

He gives two signs for false music, the natural and
the flat; and he explains that such music False
is not really false, but true and necessary, Music
for without it no *motectus* or *rondellus* could
be sung.

It became customary to colour certain notes red, and
here the rules are confusing and contradictory. Marchettus of Padua says that they either show
a change of mood, the red notes being sung Coloured
in three time values, while the black Notes
notes are in two, or they are to be sung in octaves.
But sometimes red is used to show that long before long
does not count three times, or that the second of two
breves between longs is not to be altered ; or it is used
to show that long before long is to count three times,
and breve before breve that of three semibreves. Red
is also used to vary time and mood ; where black longs
are of the value of three times, the red notes are of the
value of two ; and he naïvely remarks that in the tenor
of a certain motet in which red is used, there are
many errors ; how they are to be avoided amidst so
many contradictory uses of red notes he does not say.

Philip of Vitry says that red notes change what was
perfect to imperfect, and what was imperfect to perfect.

Story of Notation

Philip of Caserta says that if a man has not the wherewithal to write red notes, he may leave them empty. Syncope, says Vitry, is the division **Notes to be** of any figure into separate parts, as a perfect **left un-** long into three breves, an imperfect long into **coloured if** two breves.

the writer Rests are of different values, according **has no** to the number of spaces they cover: thus **paint** a rest covering one space is of the value of one time, two spaces two times, and so on; but if a rest covers four spaces it is unmeasurable. A rest **Rests** descending from a line and covering half a space is worth a semibreve, and that which rises from a line and covers half a space is a minim rest: the last two are of course our semibreve and minim rests.

He describes four points. It will be remembered that formerly notes were called points, but the point here **Points or** alluded to is what we now call a dot. The **Dots** four points are of division, of perfection, of addition, and of demonstration. We have already described on page 97 the sign which afterwards became the point of division, and whose modern representative is the bar-line, and on page 99 the point of perfection, which made perfect (*i.e.,* threefold) that which would otherwise be twofold, and is our dot after a note. " The point of demonstration is placed above a minim in major prolation,[1] and it is doubled, so that the minim stands under two dots, and after that minim one or

[1] Major prolation is equivalent to our three minims in a bar.

132

Double-tailed Notes

more semibreves must follow, and after the semibreves two more minims, and it is necessary that either the first or the last minim must have the points of demonstration, the object of which is to show that the semibreves must be sung slowly." It seems to be an elementary method of showing a *ritardando.* "The point of addition is placed behind a semibreve in major prolation, and such semibreve must be followed by a minim ; and since the point causes a minim to be added to the semibreve, it is called the point of addition." This again results in our "dot after a note"; the semibreve without a point, followed by a minim, would, according to rule, be duple, but the point of addition causes it to keep its threefold value.

Philip of Caserta doubles the tails of minims to make them equal to an imperfect semibreve; he doubles the tails and leaves the notes empty to make three minims equal to four (a triplet); and when the lower tail has a hook, four minims are equal to six.[1] The reader will recall **Minims with Two Tails** many instances of similar temporary changes in modern instrumental music. But Philip of Caserta goes on to introduce considerable complications. Thus, he adds an "empty circle" to a note and makes four minims equal in value to nine; he introduces a half-empty and double-tailed minim equal to a minim and a half, while three empty minims with single tails are equal to two.[2]

In Prosdoscimus de Beldemandis we find the "Direct" at the end of each stave, to show the

[1] See Fig. 8, p. 118.   [2] Fig. 8.

133

reader the first note of the next stave, and in mediæval times this was very necessary, since the clefs were

The Direct ever changing their lines. It was almost universal until recent times, and was required so late as 1896 in the exercises for degrees at Oxford; a curious survival of a practice the use for which had disappeared.

Prosdoscimus complains that, whereas the Italians have given up using all "points" except that of division,

Confusion in use of Dots the Gallic musicians still use many, and it is difficult to know at first sight what effect the point has. He also complains that they have a great number of different ways of showing mood and time, whereas the Italians use simpler methods.

Prolation was afterwards added to mood and time. As mood meant one long or its value in a bar, and time

Prolation meant the breve or its value in a bar, prolation meant the semibreve or its value in a bar, and it must be understood that we use the word bar merely to make the matter clear to the reader from a modern point of view. The use of bar-lines began about 1600, and was an outcome of the tablatures, to be described later. The mood was divided into major and minor, so that there were—

Major perfect mood	=	three longs	in a bar
Minor perfect mood	,,	three breves	,,
Major imperfect mood	,,	two longs	,,
Minor ,,	,,	two breves	,,

Decline of Mediæval Teaching

Perfect time	= three semibreves in a bar
Imperfect time	,, two ,, ,,
Perfect prolation	,, three minims ,,
Imperfect prolation	,, two ,, ,,

But any of these could be combined together; and in some of the treatises we have elaborate time-tables covering many pages, and reminding one of the elaborate Greek notation tables of Alypius.

John Hothby says that there are two points, those of perfection and division; and we find a general tendency as time goes on to reduce the number of points. Hothby, like Prosdoscimus de Beldemandis, gives no less than twenty-six tables of time measurements. *Points or Dots reduced in number*

An attempt is made by Coussemaker's "Anonymus IV." to show the various values of maximas by marking off the number of longs they are to contain.[1]

We have dwelt at some length on the doctrines of the mediæval Church musicians, in order to show what difficulties they had to contend with in their efforts to arrive at a satisfactory notation. The expression, "The moderns love brevity," is frequently met with, and the explanations as well as the notations gradually become shorter and simpler. *The Difficulties which had to be overcome*

By the beginning of the sixteenth century the whole fabric of moods, time, and prolation was falling to pieces.

[1] Fig. 8, p. 118.

Story of Notation

In Pietro Aaron's *Lucidario,* 1545, we find a revolt

The un-wieldy Old Teaching begins to give way before more enlightened ideas
against the old threefold measurements under "Explanation of the musical time called natural," in which he brings arguments to show that musicians are right in calling binary time natural, "in which opinion the learned John Spadaro agrees." The book was part of a dispute with Gafori, a representative of the old teaching.

The rules are collected by Zarlino in his *Istitutioni armoniche,* 1558, lest they should be lost, and by Thomas Morley in his *Plain and Easy Introduction to Practical Music,* 1597. Zarlino says that plainsong is made without any variation of time, whence it is called fixed song, *canto fermo,* as distinguished from measured music.[1]

He speaks of metrical music, which is measured in verse-metre, and which can be instrumental as well as vocal. He says that each note, beginning

Binary takes the place of Ternary Note Division
with the maxima, is *double* the value of the next below it. This is a great step in advance of the old writers, who always began with describing the threefold value, called Perfection, and treated the twofold values as of secondary consideration, being "Imperfect." Zarlino says that they are also of other values in perfect time.

[1] In England a distinction was made between "Plainsong and Pricksong," the latter referring to the notes, which were "pricked" on the parchment.

136

Decline of Mediæval Teaching

He considers that the Breve is the mother and beginning of all the other notes, since the Maxima and Longa were invented after it. Here we again have the old Greek theory of a " Primary time."

Of the three expressions Mood, Time, Prolation, he says that he intended to omit them when he began to write, as being unnecessary; but since some modern musicians might like to read some ancient Cantilena, he explains them. His words show that they had gone out of practical use in his day in favour of the two-fold note values as we know them. " If," he says, " the modern composer should not number his cantilena according to the Moods, he could really say that the matter was of little account, and that he had no knowledge of such things."

The Old Learning disappearing

The time and prolation signs, he says, were anciently cut by a perpendicular line to make the pace double, so that a breve became a semibreve and so on; or, as he says, cutting the signature was the same as making the open notes black, which reminds us that it had been discovered in the sixteenth century that both time and ink were saved by leaving the maxima, long, breve, and semibreve open (see Fig. 8, p. 118).

He gives a long description of the beat, which is derived from the pulse, and is shown by raising and lowering the hand: *levatio,* up-beat; *positio,* down-beat; or in Greek, *arsis* and *thesis.* Time was indicated by the raising and lowering of the

The Beat

Story of Notation

foot by the Greeks, hence the word "foot" for a poetical measure. Of syncopation, Zarlino says it cannot be recognised without a knowledge of the beat, and he proceeds to describe it in the form it is known to us; thus, for instance, he says a note is syncopated which commences on an up-beat and is also subject **Syncopation** to the down-beat; it consciously breaks the time and measure, and many songs become confused by too much syncopation. Morley calls the beat a "stroke," which he says is a motion of the hand. "The more stroke comprehendeth **Morley's Explanation of the Notes** the time of a Briefe, the lesse, the time of a Semibriefe." He describes the notation under the name of the Large, the Long, the Briefe, the Semibriefe, Minim, Crotchet, Quaver, Semiquaver, and explains the ligatures, Moods, Time, and Prolation at considerable length, though he says that their knowledge is practically lost. "Those who within these three hundreth yeares have **Morley regrets the loss of the Old Teaching** written the Arte of Musicke, have set downe the Moodes otherwise than they have been or are taught now in England. . . . Although it be hard to assigne the cause, yet may we conjecture that although the great Musicke Maisters who excelled in fore time, no doubt were wonderfully seene in the knowledge thereof, as well in speculation as practice; yet since their death the knowledge of the arte is decayed, and a more slight or superficiall knowledge come in steede thereof: so that it is come nowadayes to that, that if they know the

Morley's Teaching

common Moode and some Triples, they seeke no further."

He gives some examples in parts, calling the uppermost part the *Discantus*, as the Germans do now (our treble or soprano part); the second, the *altus;* the third, *tenor;* and the fourth, *bassus;* and he makes free use of ligatures. The single staves he calls verses, and at the end of each "verse" is a "Direct," which he calls an Index or Director.

If a note that should be white is written black, it loses a third of its value; this is an important rule in sixteenth century compositions. It would take us too far to follow Morley into all the complications of Major and Minor, perfect and imperfect Prolation, Time, etc., and into his long lists of proportions of all kinds in the time measurement; for those who require to solve mediæval compositions, his book, read in conjunction with the Latin writers, is very useful.

Morley's description of notes whose colour is changed

The complete scale of twelve semitones in the octave was re-established by this time. We have seen that the early Greeks had used such a scale five hundred years before our era, and that their notation was based on it; but for some reason the semitones, while being retained in the Eastern Church, were entirely lost to Western Europe in the early days of Christianity, only one diatonic scale, our A minor, with the addition of B flat, being preserved.

Re-establishment of the scale of 12 Semitones in the Octave

Story of Notation

The keyboard instruments had by this time twelve notes to the octave, and the tablatures used only one sign for a flat and a sharp; but musicians were much exercised over the necessity of making one sound do for two. We have seen that the *crux* was placed between any two notes, and was looked upon as a sort of conjunction; the *b rotundum* could also be placed between any two notes, and the *b quadrum*, our natural, was used to contradict *b rotundum*, while *b rotundum* itself contradicted the sharp. But unfortunately they were seldom written, since the singers were expected to know the rules of their application.

"False music ought not to be indicated," said an anonymous writer. In Plainsong the sharp was never lawfully admitted, though in some **The Sharp** rare cases it may be seen; and it was not **was not** required as long as Plainsong was sung **required** in unison. E flat was admitted for pur-**in Plain-** poses of transposition only; the other flats **song** were not allowed. But an occasional sharp crept into the Plainsong: one finds it very slightly indicated in the form of an elongated natural in some MSS.

With regard to the measured music, we find that while the German and Netherland musicians were very chary of writing an accidental sharp or flat, the Italians and French, on the contrary, when once they began, used them far more freely; and it appears that they were governed not so much by the effect of the chords produced, as by the melodic

Eitner's Rules for False Music

effect of the single parts. This is quite in keeping with the original sense of counterpoint, which is melody against melody, rather than a succession of pleasant sounding chords. Herr Eitner has gathered the following rules in addition to those we have mentioned on p. 117, from an analysis of later music:[1]—What are called changing notes, *i.e.,* a note standing a single degree above or below and between two notes of the same name, are generally to be made semitones; that where a note is undoubtedly a leading note, it must be raised by a sharp

French and Italian scribes were more liberal in writing False Music than their northern contemporaries

or natural; where the dominant in the bass is preceded by the note next above it (the sixth), this note must be lowered by a flat; every half or full close ends with a major chord; the answer of a fugue or imitation preserves the same intervals as the subject, so long as the tonality is not disturbed.

Additional Rules of Musica Falsa

The sharps and flats gradually found a place at the beginning of the stave, with the time signature. In early days both *b rotundum* and *b quadratum* had been used as clefs. When key signatures began to be used in the end of the sixteenth and beginning of the seventeenth century, they were naturally not so methodically applied as now. For example, if there were two F's or two C's in a

Key Signature

[1] Robert Eitner in *Monatshefte der Musik Geschichte,* vol. xx, p. 76.

Story of Notation

stave, each would be provided with a sharp, so that the key of G had this signature [musical notation], that of F [musical notation], of D [musical notation], and so on. Another peculiarity of early key signatures which we sometimes find in the beginning of the eighteenth century is the

Omissions from Signature

omission of the last sharp or flat, so that the key of E flat would be provided with a signature of two flats only, that of A with two sharps, the last flat or sharp being indicated where necessary by an accidental. This practice probably arose at a time when the importance of key relationships was not yet recognised, and was continued in some remote parts as a time-honoured custom.

With regard to accidentals, there is not even to-day universal consensus of opinion, and several dis-

Modern Dis-crepancies

crepancies of usage may be discovered by those who are interested in the matter. As long as present-day musicians understand present-day usage, these discrepancies do not matter; and since no one can make rules that will be accepted universally, we must leave posterity to make out our music as best they can.

Accidentals were formerly written before every note that was affected by them, and this practice continued to be used by some composers, even after bars were introduced. We find in Cerone di Bergamo a *Sogetto*

Double Sharps

del genere Cromatico, which (reduced to modern round notes) reads as follows :—

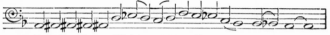

Do-mi-ne Je - su Christe, ex - au-di vo - cem me - am.

Here it will be observed that the sharp is placed before four notes in succession, and in spite of the flat in the signature, an accidental is placed before *b*. The custom of using ♯ to contradict ♭, and *vice versâ,* continued till late in the eighteenth century, though the modern use of the natural had been taught as early as 1698 by Louliè, a Frenchman.[1] **The Use of the Natural temporarily in abeyance**

With the increasing use of the complete circle of keys, a new sign for the leading note became absolutely necessary; for although at first G natural was used as the leading note in the key of G♯, this proceeding was not only un- **Double Sharps** scientific, but was misleading to singers and violinists. Hence the adoption of the double sharp, in the form of St. Andrew's cross, early in the eighteenth century, which was proposed by Mattheson. Leopold Mozart, in 1756, proposed an upright cross, and other suggestions were made (see Fig. 8, p. 118), but the St. Andrew's cross has remained in use till now.

Considerations of modulation also gave rise to the necessity for a new sign for the suppression of the

[1] "The Flat, Sharp, and Natural," by Professor Niecks, in *Proceedings of the Musical Association*, vol. 16.

Story of Notation

leading note in keys of many flats; and the double flat, as known at present, came into use about the same time as the double sharp, and, in spite of several alternative proposals, has remained in use. The conventional contradiction of these signs by ♮♭, ♮♯, is at present being discussed as unsatisfactory, and it is probable that some new sign for this purpose will be invented in the near future; though as long as musicians experience no confusion or misunderstanding it is hardly likely that any change will be universally adopted.

Double Flats

CHAPTER IX.

The tablatures — Reasons for their use — The tablature makers never adopted the ternary division of notes — Mediæval orchestras — Different tablatures in different countries — Examples from Virdung and Agricola — The bar-line nearly always found in tablatures—The dot or point of perfection—Dots of repetition—Various clefs—An organ tablature book which formerly belonged to Seb. Bach — The lute tablatures —Mace — Paulmann — Mersennus—Lute grace notes—Flute tablatures—Italian lute tablatures introduced into Spain by Narbaez—Cerone di Bergamo—Judenkunig—Modern revival of the principle of the tablature.

WHILE the Church musicians were working out a notation for voices derived from the neumes, and hampering themselves by connecting it with the Trinity, by splitting hairs over words,—such as that since *minima* means smallest, no note could be introduced smaller than the minima, or that false music must not be written down, or that since Pythagoras and Boethius say nothing about sharps, they must not be allowed, however much they improve the music, and a number of other childish restrictions,—the lutenists, virginal players, violists, organists, and others were working out and making use of tablatures, Italian *Tavolatura*, *Tabolatura*, from the wax *tabula* or tablet used for writing. This was a system, based on the same principle as the instrumental

145

Story of Notation

notation of the Greeks, of showing by letters or numbers or other means the string or fret or organ key that was to be touched, rather than the sound to be produced. We can imagine that the Church notation, with its numberless rules about perfection, imperfection, its ligatures, and other machinery, was far too clumsy for indicating instrumental music; for however well a man might be able to read a single voice part, it is scarcely possible that he could take in the time values of several parts together, as he would require to do for the organ, or lute, or clavichord. The tablature makers borrowed what suited them from the Church notation and adapted it to their needs; and an important feature in their notation is that never did they make notes worth three of the next in value, but always two, as in the earliest days of vocal measured music. They therefore had a sounder basis for time measurement to start from; and it is possible that the Church musicians were led back to the original duple significations by noticing how much more convenient the tablature method was than their own. The troubadours and minstrels of the thirteenth century, when they wrote their songs, used the square notation of the Church, and large collections of them exist in this notation; they probably extemporised the accompaniments when single instruments were used. What they did with bands of instruments, such as one sees represented

The Principle of the Tablature

The Tablature Rules were always based on Even Measure

Mediæval Orchestras

Mediæval Bands

in the fourteenth century Minstrels'
Gallery at Exeter, at Beverley (St.
Mary's Church), the twelfth century
church of St. George at Bocher-
ville, near Rouen, and elsewhere,
is not known. Perhaps they practised together until they attained
to some sort of harmony, as the
so-called village waits did till quite
recently in England. Ambros
thinks that they all played in
unison; but this is scarcely likely
when we consider the great energy
with which organum, discant, and
contrapunctus were being cultivated in the Church, and that
part-singing had reached a still
higher development outside it. It
is well known that a kind of
extempore discant was cultivated,
for which rules were made; and
hence it is not only possible, but
very probable, that the instruments
played an unwritten harmonic accompaniment to the song, and to
the leading instrument in the
dance.

We have seen that the monochord was marked with the letters
of the alphabet, and that these

MUSICIANS LEADING A TRIUMPHAL PROCESSION (ASSYRIAN).

147

Story of Notation

letters were occasionally used together with the neumes to show the exact intervals; this was the earliest form of mediæval instrumental notation; and we find letters used in the organ tablatures in Germany.

As was natural in the days when intercommunication was slow and difficult, the tablatures were not alike everywhere; each country, more or less,

Different Tablatures in different countries developed its own notation. That the Church notation was practically the same throughout Western Europe is due to the fact of its emanating from one fountain-head, Rome.

The Clavichord was a descendant of the Monochord, and was in reality merely a collection of monochords in one frame, each of which served to produce

The Clavichord three or four notes; while in its later and improved form each key had its own string. Virdung and Agricola show a clavichord and organ keyboard provided with the letters used in tablature for these instruments, starting from F below *Gamut,* which is shown by double *f;* it omits the low *f* sharp, and is lettered thus :—*g, g°, a, b,* a peculiar form of *h, c, ce, d, de, e, f, fe, g, ge, a, b, h, c, ce, d, de, e, f, fe, g, ge, b, h, cc, dd,* etc.

Time-signs standing on short lines signify rests; **Time-signs** standing over letters they signify notes. They are :—

A Breve or whole time, a lozenge.

A Semibreve or half time, a perpendicular stroke.

MINSTRELS' PILLAR, ST. MARY'S CHURCH, BEVERLEY.

Photo. : Messrs. Frith & Co. Reigate

Tablatures

A Minim is a stroke with a crook.
A Semiminim, our quaver, has two crooks.
A Fusa, our semiquaver, has three crooks; and so on.

Virdung separates all his minims, semiminims, and fusas; but Agricola and others join the crooks by horizontal lines, thus giving to a succession of quarter or eighth notes the appearance of little hurdles.

It was customary to write the "Discant," *i.e.*, the treble part of organ and clavichord music, on a five-line stave above the tablature; and on the stave the tablature signs were attached to lozenges, which afterwards became round black notes, in fact, our crotchet, quaver, etc. **The Tablature combined with the Stave**

The first thing we notice about nearly all tablatures is the use of a vertical line drawn right through them and often extending above the stave, as if the writer was determined that there should be no possibility of mistake about the measures. This line did away with the necessity of the *punctus divisionis,* and is of course the modern bar-line. One of the few exceptions to the use of the vertical line is in the organ tablatures of Arnold Schlick, 1512, described by Eitner, *Monatshefte,* vol. i. p. 114, which have no bar-lines. **The Bar-line**

The only dot used is that of perfection, which makes its note threefold, or, as we say, increases its value by half. Observe, however, in Virdung's clavichord tablature (Fig. 10, p. 150) two **The Dot**

Story of Notation

FIG. 10.

Virdung Clavichord Tablature, 1511 A.D.

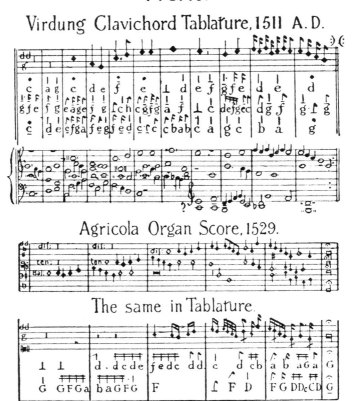

Agricola Organ Score, 1529.

The same in Tablature.

Tablatures

dots above the double bar to indicate repetition; and we shall see that dots under notes were used later for another object.

Observe the double clef in the stave, G and dd. This was very common, and in Agricola's tablature it will be noticed that there are three clefs, dd, G, and C; while in his "score" he **Double** gives a clef to nearly every line. It will **Clefs** be noticed that in the tablature he does not use the same lettering as Virdung, but the old Guidonian lettering, the lowest octave being in capitals, the middle octave small letters, and the highest notes double letters.

Grace notes are shown in the discant part of the tablature by a stroke through the lower tail of notes, as in bars four and five of Agricola's organ tablature; and, though he does not say so, **Grace** it is probable that the tilted signs in the **Notes** other parts indicate grace notes. We shall see that Mace explains how these grace notes are to be played on the lute.

Agricola gives a similar tablature for "single-voiced" instruments, such as the various kinds of viol and violin; but in them he uses the same letter- ing as Virdung does for the organ, viz. the **Viol** lowest octave underlined, the highest over- **Tablature** lined, which must have gone far towards preventing an organist from adding the violin or viol to his accomplishments (Fig. 12, p. 179). And there was a purpose in this, for these ancient practitioners were jealous of the

151

Story of Notation

encroachment of those of other trades on their own, and, like the British workman of to-day, insisted that each man should stick to his own instrument, and not earn extra pay by practising another in his leisure hours. "The French," says Morley, "who

Jealousy of Practitioners were generally accounted great masters, seldom or never would prick their lessons as they played them, much less reveal anything to the thorough understanding of the instrument."

We give examples taken from a few tablatures only, with their translations. Hundreds of tablature-books

A Bach Autograph in a Tablature-book exist in the museums and libraries of Europe, but those for stringed instruments are not all easily translated, as the writers rarely give the tuning to which they refer. Several of these books are usually exhibited to the public in the music-case of the King's Library in the British Museum, amongst them being a copy of the tablature-book of Amerbach, a predecessor of Sebastian Bach as organist of St. Thomas's, Leipzig. This copy belonged to Bach, and contains his autograph.

As the organist represented in tablature not the intervals he caused to sound, but the organ keys he pressed, so the lutenist represented the

Lute Tablatures strings and frets on which he had to place his fingers to produce the required effects; and this gave rise to certain theoretical difficulties which were overcome in practice on the unfretted violin and on the lute by playing only in a few keys. Virdung, in explaining his lute tablature, is obliged

152

Tablatures

to acknowledge that Boethius says that a tone cannot be divided into two semitones; yet the fret of the lute divides it into two semitones, and Virdung promises to explain away the difficulty at some future time. For all practical purposes, therefore, the lute was tuned in what we know as equal temperament, all the semitones being made equal, as on the modern pianoforte and organ, and it mattered nothing whether the "chromatic" intervals were called sharps or flats; in the tablature they are simply semitones.

The Theoretical Difficulties of Tuning

Moreover, it gave rise in Germany to a curious confusion of nomenclature, whereby the sharps *Cis, dis, eis, fis,* etc., were confounded with the flats *ces, des, es, fes,* etc.; and a composition in three flats was said to be in *dis—i.e.,* d sharp, while its tonic triad consisted of *dis, g, b—i.e.,* d sharp, g, b flat.

Curious German Nomenclature

The English and French lutenists usually drew six lines to represent the six principal strings of their instrument; while the bass strings, which were outside the neck, and therefore could only be played open, were tuned to the diatonic scale of C, and were represented in the tablature by the letter a, with one or more strokes against it, the two lowest strings being represented by the figures 4 and 5 (Fig. 13, p. 182).

English and French Lute Tablatures

Gerle gives the semitones by letters and figures on the joints of the hand on the principle of the Guidonian

Story of Notation

hand, and the tablature is arranged after the pictorial hand, which has two signs to each joint.

As there were several ways of tuning the six upper strings, it was necessary for the player to know first
Difficulties of the Tablature what tuning was intended for any particular tablature, and added to this was a twofold lettering—some called the open string *a*, the first fret *b*, the second *c*, and so on ; others called the opening string *o*, the first fret *a*, the second *b*, the third *c*, and so on. Others again, as Mace,[1] call the open string *a*, the first fret *b*, the second by a peculiarly shaped *c*, and so on to *y* and *k*; he explains that he uses *y* instead of *i*.

The most extraordinary lettering is that of Virdung (Fig. 12, p. 179), who explains that he learned it from a
A Blind Man's Tablature blind man, though he does not say how the blind man wrote it down, or read it when written. This blind man's name was Conrad Paulmann or Paumann. He was very celebrated in his day, and his gravestone in the church of Our Lady at Munich bears the following inscription:—
"In the year 1473, on the eve of the conversion of St. Paul, there died, and was buried here, the most artistic of

[1] *Musick's Monument ; or a Remembrancer of the best Practical Music, both Divine and Civil, that has ever been known to have been in the World*, published in 1676. Thomas Mace was a clerk of Trinity College, Cambridge, who had remarkable views as to the power of music — *e.g.*, he considers that the contemplation of concord and discord, and the nature of the octave and unison, will so strengthen a man's faith "that he shall never after degenerate into that gross sub-beastical sin of atheism."

154

Paulmann's Tablature

all masters of instruments and of music, Master Conrad Paulmann, of noble descent, of Nuremberg, and born blind, on whom may God have mercy."[1]

Agricola (whose work is in verse) mocks at the idea of a blind man teaching the tablature ; his lines may be thus paraphrased : " If a blind master teaches apprentices who can see, and, by leading them astray, makes them also blind, they must not be astonished if they get laughed at." We have copied Paulmann's tablature with exactness from the example given by Virdung (Fig. 12), and it will be observed that the translation gives the same result as that of his example of clavichord tablature (p. 150). Strings are usually numbered, either from highest to lowest, or from lowest to highest; but Conrad Paulmann uses another system. He calls the lowest string the " Great Brummer," *i.e.* Great Growler (Virdung calls it Great Prummer in his local dialect), and numbers the others from one to five. The open " Great Brummer " is marked by the figure 1 with two dots above it, the other open strings being shown by the figures 1, 2, 3, 4, 5. In the tablature the figure 2 takes the form of Z, and 5 is incomplete. Now comes what Virdung considers a very clever arrangement, but which results in the most hopeless complication. Instead of the usual method of lettering the *strings*, the blind man letters the *frets*, the first fret having *a, b, c, d, e,* for the five strings respectively, beginning with the lowest ; the second fret is lettered *f, g, h, i, k ;* the third *l, m, n, o, p,* and so on through the alphabet.

[1] Ambros, *Geschichte*, vol. iii. p. 436.

Story of Notation

When he comes to *s* he begins again with *aa, bb, cc,* etc. The Great Brummer frets are named by capital letters, corresponding with the small letters of the string above it—thus, A, F, L, Q, X, AA, etc. The tuning used is—

and the notes, taken alphabetically, instead of producing a series of semitones, as in other tablatures, have the following extraordinary result, reminding one of the curious order found in the earliest Greek instrumental notation (Fig. 1, p. 16) :—

or, if we take the semitones successively from the open D string, they produce the following arrangements of letters and figures:—

a confusion which, without lengthy explanation, it would be hopeless to endeavour to unravel.

Mace's Tablature

With regard to time-values, the Germans, of whom Agricola and Virdung are representatives, use what we may call the vertical line and crook notation; while Mersennus in France, and Mace in England, place crotchets, quavers, etc., over the tablature to show the value of the letters beneath them, it being understood that letters without notes over them are of the time of the last note that has occurred—*e.g.*, in the third bar of the quotation from Mace (p. 182), in which the final *d* is to be of equal value with the preceding *b*, *i.e.* a quaver. The dots under letters, or, as Mace calls them, the pricks, refer to the fingering, one prick for the first finger, two for the second.

Various ways of showing Time-values

Mace describes fifteen varieties of grace notes as occurring in the lute tablature, calling them "Curiosities and nicities in reference to the adorning of your play." The *shake* is marked with a dot before a letter; it is of various kinds, one of which, the "nerve shake," he cannot make, for, he says, "I have had occasion to break both my arms."

Grace Notes

The *beat*, shown by a vertical line before a letter, and the *back fall*, shown by a comma before the letter, as in bars one and two of the example, were a semitone above the principal note, and made by withdrawing the left-hand finger from the string "with a twitch," after striking with the right, similar to the left-hand pizzicato of French and Belgian violin composers of the present day. It is hardly necessary to go into details of the

Story of Notation

graces called the slur, the slide, the spinger, the sting, the double and single relish; the last grace he mentions is the "soft and loud play," indicated by so : lo : equivalent to the Italian expressions f and p. He calls it "as great and good a grace as any other."

The French players used "*battements, ports de voix, passages, tremblements, martelements, addoucissements, flattements, graces, charmes, ravissements, mignardises,*" etc., and Pretorius gives a similar list of Italian graces "which give variety to the concert and pleasure and delight to the hearers." The lute was undoubtedly cultivated to a high pitch of perfection, and those who have heard it played can well understand the charm it possessed in the days when few keys were used, and the powerful orchestra and organ and modern pianoforte had not yet asserted their pre-eminence.

French Grace Notes

The viols were usually in six parts, and a chest of viols contained two basses, two tenors, and two trebles, the uppermost viol or violin part being called the discant. Their tablature in England and France is on the same principle as that of the lute; a number of lines are drawn equivalent to the number of strings, and letters placed on them to indicate the frets of the viol, or the semitones of the violin. For the violin this was simple enough as long as only the "first position" was made use of: it must have had its inconveniences when the player wished to obtain a different effect by shifting. The violin tablature soon gave way to the use of the "French violin

Viols

Wind-Instrument Tablatures

clef," in which the G was placed on the middle line of a five-line stave, while the lower instruments used the alto, tenor, and bass clefs. The English violinists used the ordinary treble clef, as at present.

The wind instruments also had their tablatures, of which we give an example (Fig. 12, p. 179). They were divided into discant, alto, tenor, bass, and the tablature, founded on the holes to be opened (not on the sounds emitted), was the same for all, though its translation naturally varies with the pitch of the various instruments. Thus, if all the holes were closed on a discant flute, as described by Virdung, the resulting sound was the low G in the example (Fig. 12); while if all the holes of a tenor flute were closed, the result was D; and the same in a bass flute would result in gamut G. The opening of the lowest hole was indicated by the figure 1; it resulted in A on the discant, E on the tenor, and low A on the bass. There were no keys on the flute, and the fingering was complicated. Thus the highest *f* required the thumb hole half open, the 6th, 4th, 3rd, 2nd, and 1st fully open; and the scale is given by lengthy numberings, such as 8 6 4 3 2 1, 8 5 3 2 1, 8 5 4 3 2 1, etc. These are contracted into the strange forms shown in the diagram. It will be seen that here again there is no regular scale order, such as one would expect; the numbers and figures proceed according to the holes, not according to the intervals.

The Italian lute tablature was made on the principle of exhibiting the strings and frets by lines and numbers,

Story of Notation

but it complicated matters by, as it were, turning the strings upside down—that is, the lowest line of the tablature represented the highest string of the lute; the open strings were shown by o, the frets by the figures 1, 2, 3, 4, etc. The tablatures published in one country had to be translated for publication in another, as if they were books in different languages.

Italian Lute Tablature

Organ music, whether written on staves or in tablature, was called organ tablature. Thus a book recently exhibited in the King's Library, published at Venice in 1549 by Antonio Gardano, consisting of a five-line French violin and six-line bass stave, is called "Intabolatura d'Organo," and the word "Tablatur" was used in the same way in Germany.

Organ Music called Organ Tablature even when written in Staff Notation

The Italian lute tablature, by numbers, was introduced into Spain in 1538 by Narbaez for the Vihuela, or guitar. It is fully described in Spanish by Cerone di Bergamo, a priest and musician of the Royal Chapel at Naples in 1613, who explains that music was flourishing very little in Spain owing to the dearth of teachers and writers; and that, having travelled much in that country, he found many young men (*Mancebos*) anxious to learn, who could not do so for want of masters, the practitioners being unable to teach. His book is a complete treatise on measured music, and of tablatures he says:—"To-day there are two sorts of tablature in

Introduction of Tablature into Spain

160

Barbarous Tablatures

use, one starting from zero, and the other from 1; that from zero being most common. The strings have to be touched according to the numbers, o signifying an open string; 1, the first fret; 2, the second; and so on. Time is measured by notes of *canto figurato* placed over the tablature, but this only does for those who know *canto figurato;* the other way is by signs." The signs he gives are the same in principle as those of Agricola and Virdung—viz., an upright line for a semibreve, an upright line with a crook for a minim, with two crooks for a semiminim, and so on, though they are slightly different in form. Points placed near the numbers show the fingering, as in Mace's tablature. His tablature refers to an eight-stringed lute or guitar, the six first strings of which are in the same intervals as those described on p. 156, though at a lower pitch.

The tablatures had not a very long life. Judenkunig, a lutenist and violist living at Vienna, writing in 1523, speaks of that for the lute as lately invented. "It is generally known that the lute tablature has been invented within living memory." Decline of the Tablatures "There are so many extraordinarily barbarous tablatures which have arisen through inexperienced composers and common Lute-smiters, who use such bad fingering as to make the music incomprehensible, and the voices get mixed, and *mi* is set for *fa* and *fa* for *mi*. . . . Since the Tablatures have become quite common, and for this reason brought into contempt, most are wrongly written by those who do not understand them, and cannot learn them; and they make impracticable

Story of Notation

double stops, and misunderstand the measures, and mix things up so that it is impossible that any good should result from their bad fingering: if any one should practise day and night, his labour is lost, unless he thoroughly knows each letter in the tablature."

Mace, writing of the lute in 1676—viz., a century and a half after Judenkunig—seems to be reviving what was almost a lost art; the organ tablatures had long before this given way to staves of from five to ten lines, while virginal music was usually written on two staves of six lines each.

The tablatures had the disadvantage of not showing the intervals, and they necessarily differed for different instruments. By not showing the exact intervals, they were a very imperfect guide to violinists, trombonists, etc., even when few keys were used; while for distant modulations they would be impossible. Again, it was a great drawback that the notation of each instrument had to be learned separately; for no man can confine himself to one instrument.

Draw-backs of the Tablatures

The fact that a tablature was useless unless the instrument was tuned in a way to suit it, while many different methods of tuning were in vogue, was all against its continuing in favour; for it is well known that to disturb the tuning to which an instrument is accustomed throws it out of gear for a considerable time. What was required was a universal notation, suitable to all instruments, which should show the intervals, not the frets and strings; and this was found

162

A Voice Tablature

in the rapidly developing vocal staff notation. It is
remarkable that the principle of the tablature has been
revived and much cultivated in the nineteenth century
for voices, not instruments, under the name of the
"Tonic Sol-fa" notation, of which we shall speak in a
later chapter.

CHAPTER X.

WE have seen the single line scratched on the parchment grow into two coloured lines, then into a four-lined stave; and such it has remained for

Enlargement of the Stave

Gregorian music to this day. But for measured music, the number of lines was only limited by the compass of the music to be performed. Ledger or leger lines are of comparatively late invention. When first used they had a somewhat awkward appearance owing to its being thought necessary to use them both above and below

Early Scores

a "space" note outside the stave. Hence they were avoided, whenever possible, by a change of clef, especially of the C clef.

The whole of a vocal score was at first contained in one great stave, and vertical lines were often drawn through it as a guide to keep the voice parts together. These lines were not bar-lines, though they looked like them. They were placed at irregular intervals, and some-**Staves of many Lines** times marked as much as whole phrases, sometimes only single notes, and the word "score" in the modern sense of "full score," etc., has been derived from the lines thus "scored" through the many-lined stave.

In the *Early English Harmony,* published in photographic facsimile by the Plainsong and Mediæval Music Society, there are several interesting examples of scores of the thirteenth century **Early Five-lined Staves** and onwards. Curiously enough, the earliest specimen given in this publication of a score, in our sense, is a secular song in two parts, each part being written on a five-lined stave. The lower stave has the F on the fourth line, and is therefore our "bass stave," the upper has the C on the first line, and is our "soprano stave." The music is written in bold square notation, like that of the Sarum Gradual, and the composition is attributed to the twelfth century.

Then we have on Plates IX. and X. of the same publication two thirteenth-century scores of eight lines, with very irregularly placed vertical lines. The composition is in two parts, the C clef being on the fourth

165

Story of Notation

and eighth lines, so that here (and in many other mediæval scores) the lines change their names with the part that is written on them. Thus, in **Eight-lined Staves** the eight-lined stave we are referring to, the four lowest lines will be respectively D, F, A, C, and the four upper the same; but if the lower voice occasionally overflows into the upper four lines of the stave, they are temporarily treated as belonging to the lower C, so that the fifth and sixth lines become E and G instead of D and A. While if the upper voice overflows into the lower half of the stave, the third and fourth lines become b and g instead of a and c. As this practice is very common in the large staves used by mediæval writers, we give an example in modern notation to show our meaning:—

Or, to take a modern example, Brahms, Op. 10, No. 3:—

Here the lower part must be read as in the bass clef, the upper part in the treble. This use of the stave must have led to considerable inconvenience when the parts

Staves of Many Lines

crossed, or when more than two voices were employed; and we find very early that the stave was divided into two or more portions of generally five lines, though it must be remembered that, as we said in Chapter IV., p. 58, such changes cannot be attributed to definite dates, the newer methods being used concurrently with the older for centuries.

Plates XX. and XXI. of *Early English Harmony* show three-part scores of the thirteenth century of no less than fifteen lines, the fourth of which has the F clef, the eighth and thirteenth having the C clef. **Staves of Fifteen Lines** The number of lines varies from fifteen to fourteen and thirteen, and the position of the clefs is often changed. The stave is not "scored," but short vertical lines are placed at intervals within it to show the correspondence of the music with the rhymes. Vol. xxii. of the *Monatshefte für Musickgeschichte* contains a facsimile of a five-part composition on a stave of twenty-four red and blue lines, and without any vertical lines.

Leger lines being as yet unknown, the composer added a new line right across the page whenever he required to write a note above **A Stave of Twenty-four Lines** the stave he began with. One sees evidences of this in Plate XXIV. of *Early English Harmony,* where extra lines have been crowded in after the copy was begun.

Sometimes the composer or copyist did not even take the trouble to use a ruler or to "score" the stave as in Plates XXIX. and XXX. of the above work, showing

Story of Notation

extracts from a thirteenth-century three-part composition in the University Library of Cambridge, in which the fourteen lines are very irregularly drawn by hand.

The general rule in these early English scores seems to be to use eight lines for a two-voice and thirteen to fifteen lines for a three-voice composition.

The fourteenth and fifteenth century MSS. show an increasing tendency to diminish the number of lines to
five or six, and to give each voice its separate stave, changing the clef whenever necessary. By the sixteenth century we may consider the five-lined stave as practically confirmed for vocal parts, though here and there other staves were used; and as composers made all kinds of extraordinary canons, so they played tricks with the stave, writing whole movements on two lines or even one only, to show their skill.

The Five-lined Stave confirmed for Vocal Music

But though the five-lined stave gradually became confirmed for voices, the same cannot be said for instruments, especially for those with keys. Two staves of six lines were frequently used for the harpsichord in the sixteenth and seventeenth centuries; and for the organ a stave of six lines for the right hand and of eight lines for the left. That this was common in Italy is shown by a MS. book of organ pieces by divers composers in the library of the Royal Conservatoire of Music at Naples (see p. 170), in which the six- and eight-line staves are printed, the music being written by hand. The precise

Instrumental Staves

The Great Stave of Eleven

date of this book is unknown, but the compositions are by Galluccio, chapel-master at Paris in 1597; Pasquini, born 1580, organist of St. Peter's at Rome; Conversi, *circa* 1550-1600; Merulo, 1533-1604, and two unknown composers named Da Zoppa and Vandales.

There is also in this library a similar book, lithographed, containing pieces by various Bolognese and Venetian organists, having the same arrangement of staves; but in one sonata both hands have seven lines.

In this book the third sharp is omitted from the signature, and sharps are contradicted not by naturals, but by flats. The book is regularly barred throughout.

By the middle of the seventeenth century the five-lined stave was practically in universal use for instruments and voices (except plainsong), and has continued so till now, and is likely to last for many centuries. *The Five-lined Stave confirmed for Voices and Instruments*

The so-called "Great stave of eleven" is a theoretical stave which was never in practical use except by accident, as in the first of the three examples of contrapuntal

Treble Clef.   Soprano.   Mezzo-Sop.   Alto.   Tenor.

Bass Clef.

169

Story of Notation

progressions from De Muris, shown in Fig. 11. It consists of the two five-lined staves of the piano or organ,

FIG. 11.

The Claves or Clefs.

Use of Clefs in Ars Discantus by De Muris

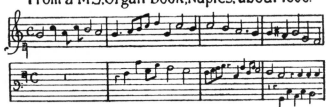

From a M.S. Organ Book, Naples, about 1600.

braced together, the middle line, C, being omitted. It will be found that by drawing two ordinary staves

Clef Forms

two spaces apart, and then filling in the missing
middle line, we have a theoretical stave of eleven
lines containing the three clefs in their proper places;
and by using the fourth to the eighth, or
the fifth to the ninth, or the sixth to the **The Great**
tenth, with the C clef always on the sixth, **Stave of**
we obtain respectively the "tenor," "alto," **Eleven**
and "soprano" "clefs"—the clef is the **Theoretical**
same in all, and on the same line, but it has
become customary to name it according to the voices
it is used for. This theory was, however, not known
to the inventors of the stave; they, like Guido, merely
placed the clefs where they found it convenient, and did
not consider that the C clef was always on the middle
line of a stave of eleven, out of which other lines were
taken as required.

The clefs have, as seen in Fig. 11, taken many forms,
and, except the G clef, have quite lost any resemblance
to the letter they represent. In the early
MSS. we rarely find the G clef used; the **Various**
C and F were by far the most usual, though **Forms of**
we find other letters used as clefs, such as **Clef**
a, or the round or square b, or d or dd. G was not
a favourite for some reason, and hardly appears till we
come to the instrumental staff notation in
the sixteenth century. In the five-lined stave **The**
it was at one time frequently placed on the **G Clef**
middle line, and was then called by English musicians
the French violin clef; in fact, the G clef was on the
Continent associated with the violin, and is called by

171

Story of Notation

the Germans the *Violin-Schlüssel,* and by the Italians *Chiave di violino.*

Except by English cathedral composers, it has been rarely used for the treble voice in choruses, the "soprano" clef, C on the first line, being used for this purpose in German scores to this day; but for solos it was frequently used for the tenor, soprano, and alto voices. Yet it has on the Continent always been considered more as an instrumental than as a vocal clef.

The C clef may occur on any of four lower lines, thus:—

It is used for soprano, alto, and tenor voices; for viola, violoncello, trombones, and bassoons in the orchestra. It frequently occurs in old-keyed instrument music, such as Handel's concertos, Bach's organ works, and the whole of the right-hand stave of the forty-eight Preludes and fugues was originally written with the "soprano" clef, while the Clavier-Uebung was printed with the "alto" and "treble" clefs.

The C Clef

English cathedral composers gave up the use of the "soprano" in favour of the "treble" clef about the end of the eighteenth century. It is used in Boyce's cathedral music (1778), for example, but in Arnold's continuation of the work, published in 1790, the G clef is used for the treble voice.

Bar-lines

In recent times the G clef has been used for treble, alto, and more recently still for tenor voices; for the last the notes are to be sung an octave lower than written, and the clef is therefore sometimes doubled thus, : a precaution very necessary where more than four parts are used, and an excellent guide to the eye of the reader in a large vocal score. A similar doubling of the G clef occurs in C. P. E. Bach's *Die Israeliten in der Wüste,* 1775, in the flute part, to show that two flutes are to be used. The F clef was sometimes placed on the middle line and called the Baritone clef.

The bar-line, though used in the tablatures absolutely regularly, and with the modern meaning, only gradually crept into voice parts, beginning to appear there about 1600.[1] It was at first irregularly placed, though there is a method in the irregularity, for it does not occur in the haphazard manner of the old "scores" across the many-lined stave.

The irregularities do not result, as one might expect, in alterations of time species from double to triple. In triple time they consist in producing a sixfold or ninefold instead of a threefold bar, by the omission of bar-lines, and in duple time the only irregularity con-

---

[1] The word "bar" first occurs in Morley's *Introduction,* 1597, p. 176, and is frequently used in the succeeding pages. The examples in the second and third parts of this work are regularly barred throughout, those in the first part being unbarred.

Story of Notation

sists in occasionally placing a bar-line so as to produce a measure of the value of a bar and a half—the result being much the same as when a composer commences his fugue with a whole duple bar, and makes the answer enter at the half bar. So that there was a method in the irregularity of the original barring, and it is possible that the composers had a finer feeling for rhythmical variety than we have, and that they, like their successors of the present day, purposely displaced the principal accent, not by introducing a single bar of less than the normal measure, but by lengthening the normal bar. Although the bar is found regularly used throughout some early seventeenth-century compositions, notably, for example, in Caccini's opera *Eurydice,* published in 1600, yet it was not established universally till the eighteenth century. Thus in a

Gradual adoption of the Bar-line book of Duos for solfeggi by Christofori Caresana, published at Naples in 1693, no bar-lines are found: even in an educational work, entitled *Elementorum Musicæ Praxis,* by Gregorio Strozzio, Naples, 1683, they are absent, though in the same author's *Capriccios,* for organ or cembalo, after the subject is given out without bars, the rest of the piece is barred regularly. It would

Peculiar use of the Dot appear that bars were used in North Italy before they penetrated to the south: the compositions of Carlo Gesualdo Principe di Venosa, published at Geneva in 1613, are barred. And here we may notice a peculiarity that is found in much music of this and the next century, in

Syncopation

the use of the dot after the last note of a bar, thus lengthening the note into the next bar. The modern and more practical method is to tie the last note of the bar to the first note of the next bar. Thus:—

(a) *Principe di Venosa.*

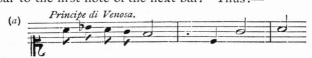

Modern method:—

(b)

The method (*a*) will be found in much old cathedral music, and is a little puzzling to those unaccustomed to it; and there is yet another ancient way of tying a note, when the first is equal to the second, by placing a white note *on* the bar-line, thus:—

equivalent to

Playford, in 1658, calls syncopated notes, such as these, "Driven notes," and the dot, the **Driven** "Prick of perfection and addition." He **Notes,** also describes "tyes or holds" to show **Prick of** that one syllable is to be sung to two or **Perfection** more notes; or in violin and viol music to show that

Story of Notation

several notes are to be played with one bow. His full close is indicated by the sign ⌢, called by us a pause. In the nineteenth edition of his book, published in 1730, the editor speaks of "the new tyed note,"

The "New Tyed Note" referring to the modern forms given in the two foregoing examples; and he also mentions as a novelty the tying of quavers thus ♩♩♩, instead of ♪♪♪

In 1658 the circle was still used as a time-sign, but Playford gives each time-sign a figure. Thus:—

Slow Disappearance of the Moods

Perfect of the more mood, $\odot_3$;

Perfect of the less mood, ϕ_3;

Imperfect of the more mood, $\mathbb{C}_2$;

Imperfect of the less, ϕ_2.

The word mood is here used in the sense of prolation, referring to the minims, not the breves in a measure. His sign for repetition is the letter S with dots, thus:—:§:

Adlung, in 1758, speaks of the circle with a dot and circle with a line as rapidly disappearing, being unnecessary now that bars were universal; but the great C he says is still used for a semibreve or its value in a bar, the other time signatures being fractions of a semibreve $\frac{2}{4}$, $\frac{4}{4}$ (equivalent to C), $\frac{6}{4}$, etc. He says that the lower figure indicates the kind, the upper the number of notes in a bar. Pretorius had in 1618 proposed little strokes, answering to the bar-line.

The so-called double bar has been in use from the

176

French Names of Notes

earliest times: it is the "rest" which marks the end of
a complete period, and is coeval with the
other rests. As it does not mark the end of
a measure, and as a complete period rarely
ends with a complete measure, the double
bar occurs, and always has occurred, in any part of a
measure.

The
Double
Bar

The repetition dots appear very early in instrumental
music; we see an example in the tablature (p. 150),
whence they were incorporated into the staff
system. For the repetition of a Plainsong
passage the Roman figure II. was used, or
III. if it was to be sung three times, as in the Kyrie.

Repetition
Dots

The *Fermata* sign, called "pause" in England,
appears very early in both measured music
and tablatures, to indicate dwelling on a
note beyond its normal value: it has never
changed its shape.

The
Pause

Under the influence of the tablatures the old complicated system of Moods, Times, and Prolations
gradually disappeared, as we have seen; and Prolation
became Proportion or Time; the semibreve became the
fundamental note, the minim the half note, the crotchet
the quarter note, and so on; and these are the names
they now have in Germany. French musicians, looking
to their shapes, name the notes ○ *ronde,* ♩ *blanche,*
♩ *noire,* ♪ *croche* (while they apply the word *crochet* to
the hook of the quaver), ♪ *double croche;* and Italians
use the old Latin names, *Semibreve, minima, semi-*

177

Story of Notation

minima, croma, semicroma. Attempts have been made in America and England of late to use the German method of nomenclature, on the ground that it is illogical to call the chief note a *half short* (semibreve), when no whole short or long are in use; but so far the attempts have not met with any great success.

The influence of the tablatures produced a conflict between theory and practice in perfection and imperfection of measures, which ended in the

The Broken Circle

gradual disappearance of the circle as a time signature, while the broken circle, used at various times to indicate Imperfect Mood, Imperfect Time, and Imperfect Prolation, now became the sign for the measure of the semibreve, the bar of one semibreve or two minims or four crotchets in value; and the shape of the broken circle, in conjunction with the fact that duple is the most frequent kind of time, gave rise to the name "Common Time" in England.

Thus $\frac{3}{2}$ signifies that the bar is to the semibreve as three is to two; in other words, it is to be three halves of a semibreve—*i.e.*, three minims:

Explanation of Modern Time-signs

$\frac{3}{4}$ that it is to be as 3 is to 4, or three-quarters of a semibreve—*i.e.*, three crotchets: $\frac{6}{8}$ that it is to be six-eighths of a semibreve—*i.e.*, six quavers; and though in arithmetic $\frac{3}{4} = \frac{6}{8}$, there is a complete difference in the accentuation of bars thus represented, as all musicians know. But the differences of accentuation were not shown so simply in the seventeenth century, and we find $\frac{3}{2}$ placed

Tablatures

FIG 12.

Virdung Lute Tablature.

Agricola Discant Violin and Viol Tablature.

Virdung Discant Flute Tablature.

179

Story of Notation

where the sense of the music requires $\frac{6}{4}$, $\frac{3}{4}$ instead of $\frac{6}{8}$, and so on: for these composers, though they felt the accent, had not yet arrived at indicating it, and were still more or less under the influence of the moods and prolations. Kircher, in 1650, gives only two time-signs, saying, "Musical time is nothing else than a certain determined quantity of lesser notes contained in a breve or a semibreve. It is double perfect and imperfect; perfect time is shown by a circle, and indicates that each breve is equal to three semibreves, thus $O\frac{3}{2}$; but when this sign $\mathbb{C}\!\!\!\!\frac{3}{2}$ is placed at the beginning of the song, it indicates that the breve is imperfect and equal to two semibreves."

The square and lozenge notation died hard. In a book of motets by Carlo Guiseppe San Romano, printed

Square and Lozenge Notes

at Milan in 1670, we find open square breves, lozenge semibreves, and minims. The signature C $\frac{3}{2}$ indicates that the measure consists of two dotted breves—*i.e.*, of two breves (imperfect measure), each of which, being dotted, contains three semibreves, and this is borne out by the barring. If such a measure existed now, we should indicate it by $\frac{6}{1}$. In the "Passion" by J. M. Trabercus, chapel-master at Naples in 1635, we find square notes and no bars; the words of Jesus are given black notation, which was obsolete at that time except for plainsong, and the ligatures that occur are confined to two notes. As late as 1676, in a book of cantatas and canzonettas by Legrenzi, we find the old black notation used to show syncopation, the three-

180

" Eurydice "

time bars being noted thus : ◌ ◌, equivalent to our ◌ ◌ , but where there ◌ is no syncopation, both notes are white ◌ ◌. But the square notation and the two-note ◌ ligatures were not yet doomed. We find them in full use in Fux, *Gradus ad Parnassum,* printed at Vienna in 1725, and again, nearly sixty years later, in the *Esemplare o si saggio di contrappunto,* by Giambattista Martini, which has been referred to on p. 111.

In Caccini's *Eurydice* it is curious to see all *fioriture* written out in single lozenge-shaped semiquavers—*i.e.,* the strokes through several notes which were used in the tablatures did not yet **"Eurydice"** obtain in voices (see p. 176). Sometimes as many as thirty-nine such semiquavers occur on one syllable, and the composer must have given plenty of time to the writing down of his compositions. That the inconvenience of writing numbers of lozenges hastily was early felt is shown by a composition of Dufay in the Bodleian (1400-1474), published in facsimile by Mr. J. F. R. Stainer, where the lozenge becomes an open triangle to save time. Lozenge notes are still used in the hymn-book of the Reformed Dutch Church.

In seventeenth and eighteenth-century instrumental music it was not uncommon to indicate so-called common time with a large 2, and three **Inconsist-** crotchets in a bar by a large 3 in the stave, **encies in** as in Rameau's *Pièces de Clavecin* with **Time** violin and violoncello, printed in 1741. But **Signatures** this is not consistent: for if the large 2 refers to two

181

Story of Notation

minims, the large 3 ought to refer to three minims. However, as long as the player understands what he

FIG. 13.

Mace Lute Tablature, 1676 A.D.

Agricola Lute Tablature 1529 A.D.

has to count, the matter does not seem very important. Gregorio Strozzio, in his *Elementorum Musicæ Praxis,*

Leger Lines

after describing the moods and times and prolations with their mediæval signs, gives a long list of "proportions," including not only the time signatures in use at present, but a number of impossible ones, such as $\frac{4}{3}$, $\frac{5}{6}$, $\frac{7}{5}$, $\frac{7}{6}$, $\frac{8}{7}$, $\frac{8}{9}$; apparently he thought it his duty to complete all the possible combinations of figures without reference to their sense regarding music; for he makes $\frac{4}{3}$ indicate four minims, $\frac{6}{5}$, six semibreves; $\frac{8}{7}$, four semibreves; $\frac{5}{3}$, two breves and a half. He had not found the right way of expressing musical proportion. Strozzio's "Proportions"

One of the peculiarities in early leger-line notes is that they frequently had lines above as well as below them— (see p. 164); and another is, that with two staves a long way apart, the middle C, middle d, and middle b were sometimes placed midway between the two staves, looking as if they were meant for other notes, with some of the leger lines omitted by a printer's error. They are not easy to read, since it is difficult to know to which stave they belong. Early Leger Lines

About 1600 there arose a new form of tablature called in Italian *Basso continuo*, in English, *Thorough bass*, *Figured bass,* in German, *General-bass*, and in French, *Basse chiffrèe*, which was intended to indicate chords by means of figures placed over the bass notes; for the new art of harmony was now beginning to be cultivated alongside, or to the exclusion of counterpoint. Caccini's *Eurydice* is Figured Bass

Story of Notation

" figured " throughout, and it soon became the fashion to accompany everything, vocal or instrumental, on the harpsichord from a figured bass; even if there was a harpsichord or organ part in the score fully written out, a second harpsichord or second organ would fill in the chords from figures; and if in performance we find some seventeenth-century compositions thin, it is often probably because we have omitted to fill in the thorough bass chords on a keyed instrument. The idea rapidly spread all over western Europe: from the early part of the seventeenth century all full scores contained a " figured bass " part as a matter of course, and solos for voices and instruments were provided with a bass with figures, from which the accompanist was expected to fill in the harmonies according to rule.

Its decline was as rapid as its rise. By the latter part of the eighteenth century we find little music published with figured bass in northern **Decline of** Europe, though it still lingered in Italy. **Figured** By the middle of the nineteenth century the **Bass** art of figured bass playing was lost except amongst cathedral organists, who are obliged to accompany from old scores; and the system is only now retained for purposes of teaching the elements of harmony. It had this inherent defect—that no one who had not heard a composer play from his own figured bass parts could know the precise effects he produced or intended, and when the composer was a Bach or a Handel, the ordinary performer could hardly be expected to treat the harmonies with adequate skill. Moreover,

Figured Bass

there is reason to believe that Bach would improve, where he thought it necessary, on the harmonies given by the figures even of another composer; and after Handel's death the tradition accompanying his compositions was soon lost.[1]

For delicate effects in opera or oratorio, one often sees in an old score the expression *senza cembalo,* meaning that the harpsichordist is to cease filling in the harmonies, and leave the instruments and voices to do it. Again, one sees in the accompaniments to solos *tasto solo,* meaning that the harpsichordist is to play only the written notes, and not to fill in the harmony; but so inveterate was the habit between 1650 and 1750 of using thorough bass that we frequently find passages marked *tasto solo* or *senza cembalo* figured, though the figures are to be ignored in the performance!

Senza Cembalo

This form of tablature was also used in what is called "dry" as opposed to "accompanied" recitative, the chords here being filled in on the violoncello instead of the harpsichord. The practice died out at the beginning of the nineteenth century; we find it used by Mozart in *Nozze di Figaro,* 1786, but not by Beethoven in *Fidelio,* 1805.

Dry Recitative

---

[1] The idea of indicating chords by figures is ancient, for we find it in a treatise by Lionel Power to indicate Faburden. The figures for the most part indicate a succession of first inversions of triads. The treatise is one of the earliest musical works in the English language, dating from the early part of the fifteenth century. Hawkins and Burney quote from it, and the latter gives a bass passage with Power's figures.

CHAPTER XI.

By the beginning of the eighteenth century the tablatures were rapidly falling out of use, and in the ordinary
notation the round- and oval-headed notes
had taken the place of the lozenges and
squares, though there were exceptional sur-
vivals of the latter, as in Martini's counterpoint. The rests had taken the shapes that
are familiar to us, and the sharp and flat
and natural were used in the modern way,
though composers still sometimes omitted the last
sharp or flat in a signature, using two flats for the key
of E♭, no flat for the key of D minor, and so on; there
is an example in Bach's cantata, *Gleich wie der Regen,*
the aria "Mein Seelenschatz ist Gottes Wort" being
in the key of E♭, while the signature shows only B♭
and E♭.

**The Estab-
lishment
of the
Modern
Forms of
Notes**

Bach's use of the G Clef

In this cantata, and elsewhere, there is an unusual use of the G clef, peculiar to Bach, which at first sight appears extremely unscientific, but a closer examination reveals its ingenuity. The two flute parts are written on a stave provided with the G clef on the first line. There is no signature, and they play in octaves with **A peculiar use of the G Clef by J. S. Bach** the first and second viola throughout the cantata whenever they are employed. But their music is written on the same lines and spaces as that of the violas; and wherever the violas have a natural the flutes have a sharp, though the accidental flats are alike in all four parts. It looks as if the G was not used in the sense of a clef at all, and that the flutes are to read as from the alto clef, but an octave higher. This is not, however, the case; by an exception Bach here writes for a *flauto traverso* in B♭, instead of a *flûte-à-bec* in F, as was his usual custom, though the parts are only marked *flauto* in the score, and the performer is left to discover by the notation which instrument is to be used.

We have already referred (p. 53) to the Romanian letters found in some of the very earliest neumatic graduals. After them there seems to have been no attempt to introduce expression **Signs of Expression** signs for many centuries; composers were too much occupied with the notation to think of minor details. It was difficult enough to establish a system which would enable singers to read the notes quickly and easily. Moreover, the learned writers of the

Story of Notation

Middle Ages were occupied with discussing the old Greek and the Church modes, the writings of Boethius, the never-settled question of whether the interval *mi fa* was a semitone or something less, and were building up a lasting system of counterpoint and notation, so that they had no thought for the refinements of music, even if they did not, as was probable, consider expression to be the means used by the profane worldly musicians to attract the multitude.

That the words of expression in use at present came from Italy is clear from their being in the Italian language. It is evident that with the in-

Modern Expression Words originated in Italy vention of music which was intended to express dramatic and emotional effects, much depended from the first on the manner of its performance; and from hints written down at the moment of teaching it to the per-

former, the step was easy to the printing of these hints on the published pages. And the more dramatic the music became with the new harmonic and orchestral effects, the greater the number of expression directions that would be used.

The madrigal writers left the tempo to the taste of the performer; light and shade, *forte* and *piano, crescendo* and *diminuendo* not only were unknown to them, but are not an advantage if introduced into their works. We have seen that Morley mentions the expressions *so, lo,* for soft, loud. The Italians began about the middle of the seventeenth century to freely use the words *piano* and *forte* for this purpose, and gradually

188

Words of Expression

increased the number of signs, which are still increasing.

As early as 1638 we find in some of the lute books directions for *piano* and *forte*, the sign **V** for *mezzo-forte;* ⟍ ⟋ for *crescendo* and *diminuendo; p, f,* and the words *presto, adagio,* etc. These were at first used for instruments more than for voices. They were, of course, less used on the harpsichord and organ than on other instruments, as these instruments were only capable of producing change of power by changing stops or manuals. Bach, in his organ music, uses very few expression signs, but he frequently indicates change of manual. Handel also uses few except *f* and *p.* The means of expression have improved, especially with the invention of the piano, and are improving still.

The old English composers used English words for expression, and Schumann introduced the fashion of using the German language. It is, however, more convenient, on the whole, to adhere to Italian, since musicians almost universally understand its musical terms.

English and German Words of Expression

Ornaments largely increased in number at the beginning of the eighteenth century, and it is often difficult to translate them into modern notation. So strong was the habit of introducing them that J. S. Bach gives shakes to the oboe in positions in which they cannot be performed.

Ornaments

The ornamental signs are now reduced to two, the shake and the turn; but it is becoming more and more

189

Story of Notation

customary to write the turn in full, and the sign used for it will probably soon be obsolete. The older school of English organists, who constantly introduced unwritten ornaments, has scarcely yet died out.

The *staccato* sign first appeared in the works of Couperin, Sebastian Bach, and Rameau, in the form of dots over notes. By J. C. Bach it is used **The Staccato Sign** as a dot or an upright stroke, according to the degree of staccato required, but at the time of its appearance no explanations as to its use were given. The *legato* sign was used early in the eighteenth century, and the staccato and legato in **The Legato Sign** combination first appear in Mozart's works. Jomelli was the first who used crescendo and diminuendo in other than lute music.

Expression signs enormously increased in number during the course of the nineteenth century, owing to the rapid development of the emotional side of instrumental music, and the improvement of instruments, especially of the pianoforte. Not all the signs of expression used by eighteenth-century composers have become universal. For instance, Couperin introduced a kind of inverted pause, $\curvearrowright$, to indicate that the player was to slightly delay before striking the note, which has disappeared from use.

Amongst the latest nineteenth-century signs are the underlined staccato, and the vertical line used by Westphal to indicate the phrasing; but these have not yet come into general use.

Byzantine Music

We must now go back for a moment to the Middle Ages to refer to a form of notation which seems certainly to be derived from the same origin as ours, but has developed in an entirely different direction, and which is still in use in Europe, though destined to succumb **Notation of the Greek Church** some day before the more practical and universal staff notation. It will have been noticed that we have frequently used the expression "Western Europe" in connection with notation. The music of the Greek Church did not develop on the same lines as that of the Western Church; on the contrary, it never lost the chromatic tetrachord, which is still one of its most important features, and is regularly used in the Mass.[1]

The Rev. S. G. Hatherley, in his *Treatise on Byzantine Music* (1892), says : " The music, sacred and profane, of the Eastern nations, Christian **Eastern European Music based on the Old Greek Chromatic Scale** and non-Christian, within and adjoining the old Byzantine Empire, is based primarily upon the chromatic genus, containing two semitones in the tetrachord.[2] The diatonic genus, containing one semitone only in the tetrachord, is also in use, but is seldom sustained exclusively for any length of time in practice, being blended, sooner or later, to a greater or lesser extent, with the chromatic genus." The

[1] *E.g.*, in the Liturgy of St. Basil.
[2] That is to say the chromatic tetrachord described in Chapter I. ; not the succession of semitones called by us a chromatic scale.

Story of Notation

music of the Eastern Church is always sung unaccompanied, and it is therefore not bound to the twelve sounds in the octave given by the organ; on the contrary it is free as to intonation, and therefore it is only capable of being represented by the staff notation on the understanding that the thirty-one signs used in our notation in an octave really represent thirty-one different sounds, and not the twelve equally tempered sounds of the organ: or perhaps it will be clearer if we say that some of the varieties of tuning described in Chapter II. are still in use in the Greek Church, and in Eastern Europe generally; and not only these features, but the modes of ancient Greek music can be heard, both in Greece and, strange to say, among the peasants of Brittany.[1]

It will be seen therefore that the music of Europe developed not in one direction but two: the Western musicians, rejecting all but the one diatonic scale, applied to it the combinations described by ancient Greek writers, and built up a system first of organum then of discant, which led to counterpoint and harmony, for which a simple pictorial notation was a practical necessity; the Eastern musicians adhered to the old scales, and only comparatively recently introduced harmony under the influence of the Westerns,

European Music has developed in two directions

---

[1] The writer, on first hearing the Breton peasants using the modes in dance music, thought they were influenced by the Church modes; but M. Bourgault-Ducoudray finds that their music is older than the Church, and goes back to pre-Christian times.

Pachymère's Treatise

since which they have been compelled to use Western notation.[1]

The Greek alphabetical notation continued in use for centuries after it was forgotten in the West, its last representative being George Pachymère, of whom Vincent[2] says: "The *Treatise of Music* of George Pachymère, which we **George Pachymère** publish for the first time, may be considered, in spite of the little attention that has till now been paid to it, as one of the most interesting that we possess on the subject. . . . In the thirteenth century, during the first half of which our author flourished, although the principles of modern music had already taken strong root, since the eleventh century had produced Guy of Arezzo, the traditions of ancient music were still living amongst the Greeks; so that G. Pachymère, who was imitated or copied by Manuel Bryennius, may be considered as the link between the ancient and modern epochs." We have shown, however, that the traditions of genera and mode are still in use in the East. The method of notation of that time has continued to the present day. It is an adaptation of the neumes, exceedingly complicated and difficult to a Western

---

[1] "In Russia the ritual books were all called in at the beginning of the seventeenth century; and a uniform Liturgy was established, in which the modern method of writing music was received. But in the Greek isles a notation peculiar to its inhabitants is still in use, which is not only as different from ours as their alphabet, but totally unlike that in the ancient missals."—Burney, vol. ii. p. 46.

[2] *Notices des MSS. de la Bibliothèque du Roi.* Paris, 1847.

Story of Notation

musician, but it seems able to express the variations of tuning better than our own notation.

Villoteau, one of the *savants* sent to Egypt by Napoleon I., has given a complete account of the **Villoteau** notation of the Greek Church, his knowledge being partly derived from observation, and partly from lessons given him by a Greek musician.[1] The subject is too complicated to be entered into here; but the general principles seem to be founded on those of the neumes, and the notation is the same as that given in facsimile by Hawkins, vol. i. page 390, of a Greek musical MS. of the eleventh century, and on pages 394, 395, which could probably be translated with the help of Villoteau's explanations.

At the beginning of every composition, and at every change of key, the sign ⌣ , called *ison,* unison, is placed, and it is followed by very complicated **The** figures, each of which has its own name. **Principles** A major second above *ison* is shown by a **of Modern** horizontal line —, probably the virga of the **Greek** neumes; a major third by the same sign **Notation** slightly inclined upwards; again, probably the virga. The apostropha, ⬎, indicates a descent of one degree, and a double apostropha, ⬎, a descent of two degrees. Here we have a direct outcome of the principle of the grave accent showing a descent. The signs all refer to *ison,* which may be any note of the scale; and they indicate intervals, but not with the exactness of Western notation. There are signs for rests and for

[1] Villoteau, *De l'État actuel de l'Art musicale en Égypte,* 1812.

Eastern and Western Notation

time, but the latter do not show relative times as with us: merely that a sound is to be shorter or longer than its predecessor.

But Western civilisation has now overshadowed Eastern Europe, and all popular music published at Athens is written in our notation. Hatherley, in his exhaustive book on the modern Byzantine scales, never uses any other; but his signatures look strange to the Western eye, owing to the fact that they indicate chromatic tetrachords, rather than key, in the Western sense.

CHAPTER XII.

ATTEMPTS TO INVENT NEW FORMS OF NOTATION, AND TO REFORM THE OLD.

New notations—Improvements come gradually—New notations appeal to the intelligence rather than to the eye—Sebald's proposal—T. Salmon—Souhaitty—J. J. Rousseau—Demotz de la Salle—Jacob—Abbé de Cassagne—Rohleder's keyboard—Labatut—Dr. Natorp—Galin—Iue—Claviere—Striby's " Universal System "—Delcamp—L. Danel—Craig's Octave System—Meerens—J. Stott—A " new " notation—Notation for the blind—Galin-Paris-Chevé—The Tonic Sol-fa notation.

THE reader will remember that we referred on p. 5 to the efforts of those who wish to improve or supplant the existing notation. If the shelves of the various libraries of Europe were searched, it would probably be found that for some centuries a new notation has appeared about every three or four years, each of which is called by its author " The " new notation, for he fondly thinks that it will become universal.

New Notations

A notation is like a language ; it does not suddenly appear, as the result of the efforts of some mighty genius. It is the result of the united efforts of generations of musicians endeavouring to express their melodies in such a way as to make them understood

196

Welsh Harp Tablature

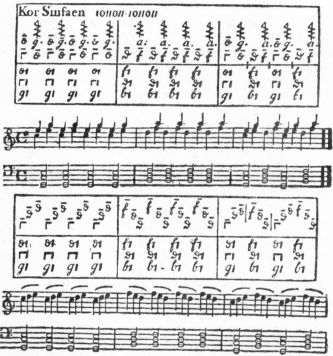

MOST ANCIENT SPECIMENS OF WELSH HARP TABLATURE EXTANT, WITH TRANSLATIONS
IN MODERN NOTATION. (From Burney's *History of Music*.)

(The signs are derived from the alphabetical notation of the Church,
except that the note C is indicated by a Greek gamma. The pitch of
the letters is shown by the little lines above or alongside them, the
curious figure above the highest notes being apparently used to show
the highest octave. The right-hand tablature is separated from the
left by a horizontal line, and vertical lines indicate the bars.)

Story of Notation

by their fellow-musicians. A composer is naturally anxious that others besides himself should have the benefit of the offspring of his mind. He does not make use of a means of expressing it that can only be known to his pupils or his immediate acquaintance: he wishes it to be spread abroad, and therefore writes it in the way that he thinks will be understood by the greatest number of musicians; or, if he does not, his admirers do it for him. Any improvements in a universally accepted notation come very slowly, not as the result of one man's inspiration, but by a consensus of opinion that such and such a detail requires to be, and can be, improved. The change from square and lozenge notes, for instance, to round ones took some centuries to complete; it was not the result of some one's suggestion, but a requirement of rapid writing; the joining of quavers was found convenient in the tablatures as a means of dividing the various parts of the bar, and was gradually adopted in the staff notation. The shapes of notes were frequently altered by individual teachers in the Middle Ages, yet the general consensus of opinion arrived at certain generally accepted forms, and rejected individual suggestions.

Improvements come gradually

Notation is an alphabet, and a far more universal alphabet than that which represents speech; for musicians in all parts of Europe can perform each other's compositions at first sight, when they certainly would not in every case understand each other's language. Hence all efforts at providing "new"

198

New Notations

notations are bound to meet with the same fate as the "universal" language called *Volapük,* which nobody has ever spoken. But no history of notation would be complete without some reference to the efforts of individuals to invent new ones, or to make radical changes in the old. To mention all would require a whole book on the subject.

Two things are generally aimed at: either the abolition of the clefs, or of the signs of sharps, flats, and naturals; and it is a remarkable fact that nearly all the new notations require a constant appeal to the intelligence rather than to the eye, showing that they result from the failure of grown persons to learn the old notation; for the grown person finds it easier to apply his intelligence than to learn a mechanical operation, while with a child the reverse is the case. The reading of the ordinary notation being an almost purely mechanical operation, presents no difficulty if acquired in early childhood, and leaves the mind free to attend to expression, which it could not do if hampered with the effort of merely reading the notes; and none of the new notations present an instantaneous picture of the position of the notes with regard to the scale.

New Notations appeal to the Intelligence rather than to the Eye

In 1529 Sebald Heyden, rector of St. Sebaldus at Nuremberg, published in Latin and German a work called *Musicæ Stichoisis,* in which he proposed to abolish the clefs, using a stave without them, with figures or words for the notes.

Sebald's Proposal

Story of Notation

In 1673, T. Salmon, a Master of Arts of Oxford, endeavoured to do away with the old clefs by making new ones: B for bass, M for mean, T for treble. The notes were to be the same on each stave, but the mean stave was to be an octave above the bass stave, and the treble an octave above the mean; and the stave was to be of four lines only. This is of course on the same principle as using the G clef for the tenor voice, on the understanding that the notes sound an octave lower than they are written. The constant change of the position of the C clef was the thing that troubled Salmon. We have reduced the changes of clef to a minimum by the use of leger lines, and some countries have almost abolished the use of the C clef for voices. But Salmon's abolition of the old clefs produced terrible confusion and far more change of clef than before, besides making a topsy-turvy picture of the tune. Matthew Locke is very sarcastic, saying, " Nor doth the transposition of the C cliff create any confusion to a beginner, as you vainly allege; for vocal music is seldom learned by men of forty or fifty years old, but by those that are young, whose voices are proper to the treble, and by that cliff only are taught; nor is the C *sol, fa, ut* cliff now much used, unless in cathedral music. As to my Psalms, in four parts, I could have printed them as well in three treble cliffs, had I thought all had been so ignorant in the use of cliffs as I am assured you are. It being usual and common for men to sing those songs which are pricked in a treble an octave lower.

T. Salmon

New Notations

"Example of a Psalm :—

"The same, pricked your way":—

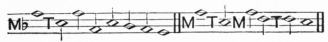

The reader will see that the great advantage of the staff over other notations—viz., its appeal to the eye, is abolished by the constant change of clef. Salmon's notation did not find acceptance.

Four years later, in 1677, a Franciscan of Paris named Souhaitty, a mediocre musician, proposed to use the numerals 1, 2, 3, 4, 5, 6, 7, for *ut,* *re, mi, fa, sol, la, si,* with rods and points attached to indicate octaves. No sharps or flats were to be shown, nor any time-signs, as this notation was only to be used for plainsong. What advantage a line of figures could have over the four-line staff and square notes of plainsong it is impossible to see.

Souhaitty

J. J. Rousseau, however, thought well of the idea, and proposed in 1743 to substitute numerals for notes; but to show the various octaves, and the sharps and flats, necessitated such an immense variety of signs that the system was more complicated than the ordinary notation.

J. J. Rousseau

The radical faults of his system were exposed by Raymond, who showed that "these simplifications will

Story of Notation

always have the defect that their simplicity and uniformity alone make them impracticable; for they do not place the musical forms instantaneously before the eyes, and appeal at the same time to the intelligence, an advantage which the ordinary notation enjoys by means of that very diversity of which its detractors complain."

Early in the eighteenth century Abbé Demotz de la Salle proposed to suppress the stave, and to use one **Demotz de la Salle** form of note only, which showed the pitch of the sound by its position; how he proposed to indicate time measure is not known, but his suggestion, if carried out, would take us back to the dark days of the neumes, before the use of lines was known.

In 1769 Jacob, a French violinist, a pupil of Gaviniés, proposed a stave without clefs, and figures for notes, in **Jacob** his *Méthode de Musique sur un nouveau Plan.* A flute-player proposed using the vowels *a, e, i, o, u, ou, eu* as notes for the major scale, though where they had the advantage over *ut, re, mi,* etc., it is hard to see.

In 1776 the Abbé de Cassagne proposed to reduce all the clefs to one only—namely, G on the second line **Abbé de Cassagne** (the treble clef), and this idea being taken up again about 1815, a good deal of music for piano was published in the "Uniclef," but it had the effect of making its users lose the power of reading ordinary music.

In 1792 a German priest named Rohleder invented

New Notations

a new keyboard, in which white and black keys were placed alternately at the same level, the black keys being equal in number with the white, and no distinction being made between E, F, **Rohleder's** and B, C. By this means he abolished **Keyboard** the naming of the notes, for all were alike; and he invented a new notation to suit the keyboard, in which the black keys were shown by black notes, the white by white notes, and values by sizes. It looks a very mechanical and simple plan, but it had so little success that it caused the ruin and death of its author. Futile attempts were afterwards made in Germany to revive it: one of its chief objections being the impossibility of seeing the intervals with sufficient rapidity on an unbroken row of black and white keys and notes.

The nineteenth century seems to have been more prolific of new notations than the eighteenth; though perhaps this appears to be the case because it is nearer to our own times, and books are better catalogued. A most remarkable effort is that of Labatut, who not only proposed to suppress the **Labatut** staves and clefs, but to make a complete notation out of a line and a circle (p. 205). We have already seen a complete notation made in the tenth century out of the letter F (p. 67). Labatut makes his notation run in octaves above and below middle G, which is his centre. All G's are represented by a semicircle, and all F's by the reverse of the G semicircle, the remainder of the notes by lines either single or in combination—

G), A V, B Λ, C |, D \, E /, F (.

Story of Notation

Time values are to be shown by attaching circles to these signs: a semibreve by the attachment of a circle with a line through it to the required note, a minim by a simple circle, a crotchet by a circle with a dot in the centre, a quaver by a semicircle, semiquaver by two circles joined making a figure 8. The various octaves are shown by the addition of horizontal lines above the signs for the higher, below the signs for the lower, notes than middle G. The sharp is to be the Greek gamma reversed, the flat to be the same inverted, the natural St. Andrew's cross. The strange shapes arrived at by these combinations are shown in Fig. 14. This notation has not obtained any large number of adherents as yet.

In 1813 a Doctor of Theology named Natorp, of Essen, used figures for the degrees of the scale, placing **Dr. Natorp** them above and below a single line, and diversifying their sizes to show the octaves. For values he combined the figures with the ordinary notation, and his book was successful enough to run through five editions.

In 1818 Pierre Galin, a Professor of Mathematics at the Lyceum of Bordeaux, and at the blind school in the **Galin** same town, published his *Exposition d'une Nouvelle Méthode pour l'Enseignement de la Musique,* which Fétis criticises thus: "There is in this work a very remarkable philosophical spirit; and the clearness of the ideas, the order of their connection, and the style, make this work a distinguished pro-

New Notations

FIG. 14.

Labatut's Notation.

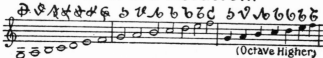

(Octave Higher)

Sharp ⌐ Flat ∟ Double Sharp �7 Double Flat ц Natural x

Striby's Universal Notation.

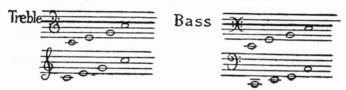

Treble   Bass

Delcamp's Notation.

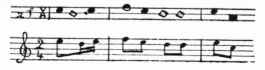

Stott's Notation.

Key A

Story of Notation

duction, whatever opinion may be held of the utility of its method."

Galin reduces the diversity of signs, and abolishes the clefs. With this object he gives a stave without a clef, provided with numbers or notes to which the teacher points with a stick while singing some well-known air. This stave is called by its inventor a "meloplast," and is used on something of the same principle as the Guidonian hand, the fingers and joints of which were pointed to by the teacher.

It will be noticed that the clefless stave had been invented several times before. Galin was so convinced of the effectiveness of his method as to assert that a child of seven to nine years of age would learn to sing anything by it in eight months, or a child of twelve in five months; on which Fétis says, "Galin was an honest man, but a mediocre musician, and was full of illusions as to the apparent success of his school. In reality, for more than forty years, not a single musician of any value has been formed on the method of the meloplast, though the schools in which they teach it are very numerous."

In 1824 Edward Iue modified the system of Galin, reducing all the scales to one, altering the shape of

Iue the notes, but he confesses that it is always necessary to refer to the ordinary notation in connection with his system.

About 1848 I. Claviere, a Frenchman, published a *Méthode élémentaire, ou Principes méthodiques de la Musique en Chiffres arabes, à l'Usage du Chant popu-*

206

New Notations

laire. This is merely another attempt to substitute figures for notes on one line; higher and lower octaves to be indicated by dots; only one key to be employed, and the major and minor **Claviere** modes, and only two kinds of time. Rests are to be expressed by O. The method is intended for uneducated people. After working for many years at his system, Claviere died at Pavia in 1851.

In 1857 William Striby, an Englishman living in Paris, published a " Universal System " (Fig. 14), in which two staves of six lines each contain notes of the same names, but two octaves **Striby's** apart. The fourth line, on which the clef **"Universal** stands, is thicker than the others; there **System "** are two clefs, treble and bass. This system does not appear to have been known beyond its author's immediate circle of friends.

Three years later, in 1860, Maurice Delcamp, in conjunction with a colonel in the French army, invented a new notation, derived from the square **Delcamp** notation of plainsong, but with notes of various shapes (Fig. 14). His stave is of three lines only. Sharps are shown by an upward tail, and flats by a downward tail, added to the notes. Values are shown by Arabic figures under the notes, a semibreve being 32, a minim 16, and so on. " Is it necessary to say that this extraordinary notation went to the tomb at the same time as its author?" (David and Lussy). Fig. 14 shows an example, quoted from David and Lussy's book.

Story of Notation

In 1867 a philanthropist, L. Danel, proposed to do away with clefs, staves, and all other impedimenta by the substitution of the letters D, R, M, F, S, L, B, for the notes *Do, re, mi,* etc. (an idea which was previously adopted in England by the Tonic Sol-faists), sharps and naturals being indicated by z, flats by l, values by a, e, i, o, u; rests by inverted letters.

L. Danel

During the last few decades English inventors have not been idle. We have Mitcherd's " Easy System of Music. Music revolutionised. No flats or sharps." This is a system of five black lines arranged in twos and threes to show the black notes, the spaces between showing the white notes. The places on the keyboard which have no black notes, BC, EF, are shown by dotted lines, dividing the groups of two from those of three black lines. One clef only, the G, is placed on the line that represents D♯, though no clef is really required. This system is really a tablature, with the defect of the tablature that it does not indicate key-relationship. It is therefore useless for vocal, and for most other music.

The " Broad Line Staff," invented by W. Lundie, consists of three lines and four spaces, enclosed between two thicker lines, which complete a stave of five lines. The middle line is always C, the lowest space always G, the highest F. No note is placed on the broad lines, since a new octave commences with the first space above or below them. The G and F clefs are used on the C line to show treble and bass; and

New Notations

thick or thin leger lines are to be added as required. This system has the defect of breaks in the continuity of the scale at every broad line, so that the eye, accustomed to successive intervals on lines and spaces, is deceived, and a mental effort is required to sing or play a single scale degree, where the apparent distance is that of two degrees. There is also the objection that applies to all these easy methods, that a person learning it is as much incapacitated from using the ordinary notation as the ordinary musician is incapable of using the easy method.

The "Chromatic Stave or Piano Tablature" is another attempt at arranging the lines and spaces to correspond with the black and white keys of the piano. It embraces the whole of the keyboard, and the different octaves are shown by substituting Arabic figures for clefs. A new alphabetical nomenclature is introduced, the spaces being named *c, d, e, f, g, a, b*, the lines *i, j, k, l*.

Craig's "Octave System of Musical Notation" consists of a five-line stave, the fifth of which represents the same note as the first, but an octave higher. Here, instead of three clefs, no less than six are used, F, G, A, B, C, D, which always refer to the lowest line of the stave; and these letters are printed in Italian type for treble, in Roman type for bass. Three of the lines are red, two are black. In any given composition one clef only is used for both staves, which are to be read two octaves apart. As in the "Broad Line Notation" the

Craig's Octave System

209

Story of Notation

thick line showed no note, so here several of the spaces show no note. Hence the same defects appear in both systems.

In 1873 Meerens proposed a "Simplified" notation. The lowest line of a five-line stave always represents

Meerens C. Roman figures representing the various octaves are substituted for the clefs,[1] and as the inventor expects future pianos to extend to eleven octaves, he numbers them from I. to XI. He proposes to reform the time signature by giving as the lower figure the required metronome number, the upper figure showing the number of beats in a bar.

J. Stott, about 1885, invented an "Improved Staff Notation" (page 205), on somewhat the same lines, his

J. Stott lowest line always representing G. Only one scale is to be used, for which seven symbols are provided, each showing by its form its relation to the keynote. Accidental sharps and flats, but no contradictory signs, are to be used.

Instead of a figure over a metronome figure, as given by Meerens, the inventor gives a figure over a crotchet, a quaver, or a minim as his time signature.

Like Salmon in 1673, he proposes to abolish the clefs, and to introduce others, namely—S for soprano, C for contralto, T for tenor, B for bass. Values of notes to be shown by the number of crooks added to the stem of the note,[2] the semibreve being shown by four stems. Sharps and flats are to be shown by circles enclosing

[1] Compare the "Chromatic Stave," p. 209.
[2] Compare Tablatures, p. 149.

New Notations

various internal features, as lines and dots. Rests are as in the old system. Key to be indicated by words, as in the Tonic Sol-fa system.

The system is to be used for instrumental music with certain modifications, though however useful it might be for vocal music, if adopted, it is difficult to see what advantage it has for instruments over the ordinary notation.

In the London *Musical Courier* of January 14th, 1897, a new notation was announced as about to appear, the chief advantage of which was to be the absence of all accidentals and key signatures. On May 26th, 1898, the same journal gave some particulars of the new notation, which was invented by Mr. W. H. Thelwall, an engineer. He proposed a seven-line stave, the middle line being thicker than the rest, and representing the note C. The alternate lines and spaces are to represent semitones, and Arabic figures placed in a circle on the thick line are to be substituted for clefs; the treble octave being indicated by the figure 6, tenor by 5, bass by 4, and so on;[1] and as there are to be no leger lines there must be changes of figure whenever the music goes beyond the stave on which it commences. It will be seen at once that this notation must result in the confusion caused by constant change of clef shown on p. 201 in Salmon's notation; and the semitonic arrangement of the lines and spaces is a modification of those

A "New" Notation

[1] Compare Meerens, p. 210; Chromatic Stave, p. 209; Broad Line, p. 208.

Story of Notation

of Mitcherd, page 208, and the "Chromatic Stave," page 209. The representation of the octaves by figures had been proposed by Meerens in 1873, and since the figures in these cases really take the place of clefs, the inventor, so far from abolishing the clefs, introduces seven or eight in place of the two in ordinary use for piano and organ music, to which alone his system could possibly apply.

The latest innovation, as far as we can learn, is that of Mr. A. H. Castle, who proposes to use five different sizes of type to represent to the eye the relative dynamic values of the notes, and to indicate features of form and phrasing. As this involves no fundamental alteration of the ordinary notation, and may be of use, especially for teaching purposes, it has a better chance of success than those notations we have described.

We have reserved for the last the description of three other new notations. One of these has filled a real need to the most unfortunate of mankind. The other two being founded on practicable principles, have had considerable numbers of adherents.

The first of the three is that used by the blind, who have invented for themselves a notation in **Notation for the Blind** which groups of raised dots, differing in number and arrangement, show both scale-degree and value, accidental sharps, flats, naturals, and rests.

The second is that of Galin-Paris-Chevé, which, though it has been officially repressed, is still taught to some extent in the communal schools in Paris and

Galin-Paris-Chevé

other parts of France, as well as in the public schools
of Geneva, and in some parts of Sweden. We have
seen that Galin invented or rather reintro-
duced a numerical notation about 1818,   **Galin-**
and that he was followed by Iue, who   **Paris-**
modified his system. The system was   **Chevé**
taken up by Aimé Paris, an advocate, and a pupil
of Galin, who, in conjunction with Émile Chevé,
a doctor, and brother-in-law of Paris, published,
about 1850, a *Méthode élémentaire de la Musique
vocale,* in which the Galin system is again modified
and used in conjunction with the Guidonian syllables
as an introduction to the ordinary notation. The
pupil is taught to refer everything to the tonic, and the
printed numbers are sung to the syllables *Do, re, mi,*
etc. Octaves are shown by dots above and below the
numbers. Rests are shown by zero, time by dots after
figures, and lines above them; and the Galin-Paris-
Chevé method of indicating values has been adopted for
the Tonic Sol-fa notation. It is of course practically a
revival of the principle of the tablature, but with the
advantage of showing tonic relationship instead of only
the strings to be sounded, and probably its success is
due to this, and to the fact that Aimé Paris gave up
his profession and devoted his life to its propagation.

The third new notation which has survived its birth
is that used in the elementary schools
in England. In the early decades of the   **The Tonic**
nineteenth century Miss Sarah A. Glover   **Sol-fa**
made use of a sol-fa notation for teaching   **Notation**

MISS GLOVER.

214

Norwich Sol-fa Method

REV. JOHN CURWEN.

children to sing simple tunes at sight. Her system, which she called the "Norwich Sol-fa Method," was enlarged and improved by the Rev. John Curwen, a

Story of Notation

Nonconformist minister, and it is now very widespread, and is used for important musical work. The name "Tonic Sol-fa" was given to the improved method by John Curwen.

Like the French system, it is a kind of vocal tablature, in the sense that no attempt is made to indicate the rise and fall of the melody; but it has the advantage over the tablatures of recognising the complete series of signs used in the staff notation; in other words, it does not force the tone into a division of two equal semitones, as was the case with the old tablatures.

No system of notation with only twelve signs for the octave can have a chance of success for reading vocal music: an instrumentalist has a mechanical means at hand by which his C♯ and D♭ are forced to be represented by the same sound; a vocalist could not make the same sound do for both notes, however hard he might try.

Another advantage of the Tonic Sol-fa notation is that it refers all intervals to a tonic, on the same principle as that of the mediæval and modern Greek notation, which refers all intervals to the starting note *ison* (p. 194). The tonic is impressed on the singer's mind before starting, and provision is made for the new tonic in case of modulation, on the principle made use of by Guido for change of hexachord—namely, calling a note by two or more names. In the case of the modern Greek notation, the new *ison* is sounded by a singer appointed for the purpose. The Tonic Sol-fa consists of the Guidonian syllables *Do* (*ut*), *re, mi,* etc., reduced to

Tonic Sol-fa

their initial letters,[1] and provision is made for indicating values and accidental sharps and flats. There is only one notation for all keys; for in modulation the *do* is simply transferred to the new tonic.

Though there is no attempt at showing the rise and fall of melody in the notation itself, those who are taught to sing from it are shown a "modulator" in the form of a ladder, on which all the steps of the scale are given with the related scales, the tonic triad being made to stand out from the rest by heavier type; and the weak point in the system seems to be that the singer has the ladder taken away from him when actually putting what he has learned into practice, instead of having the rise and fall of melody always before his eyes. Moreover, it seems that the time spent in learning to read from the modulator might be more profitably spent in learning to read from the ordinary notation; and once the theory of the scale is learned, facility in reading from any notation only comes with practice. It appears therefore to be rather a waste of time and effort to learn two processes where one is sufficient.

The Tonic Sol-fa notation has had great success in England and the colonies, probably for two reasons: because it certainly is based on more scientific principles than any of the rival new notations, and because it was very energetically brought before the public by its founders at a time when there was little knowledge of music in England, and a growing desire to know

[1] Compare p. 208.

Story of Notation

more. There is reason to think that it is destined to have a considerable vogue for some time before it finally disappears from general use; and it will certainly be looked upon by future generations as one of the most remarkable musical manifestations of the nineteenth century.

Musical notation, however perfect, can never entirely represent the composer's meaning. Much must be left to the imagination of the performer, and only deep and prolonged study and experience can enable him to render the printed or written notes satisfactorily. This applies more especially to the highest class of composition; for common music, in which no artistic intelligence finds a place, will sound almost as well on a machine as when performed by a human being. The more emotion and artistic power felt by the composer, the less satisfactory is a mechanical and unintellectual performance. A machine, or a well-drilled performer, can certainly play the most complicated written notes, often with more perfection than the more intelligent but more excitable artist; but the latter will represent the composer's meaning, while the former will not, however note - perfect the performance. "Perhaps," says Schumann, "it is only genius that understands genius": certainly more is required than a mere singing or playing of the written notes; and no notation will ever supply the place of musical intelligence. Hence the source of the various "readings" of classical works; for, as in the drama, so in music, every highly skilled and intellectual performer

Conclusion

has his own idea of what the composer intends to convey. Modern music has reached an extraordinary degree of development, and there are not wanting signs that it will become still more complex; and the more it progresses, the greater the demands made on the executant.

Burney, in his *State of Music in France and Italy,* tells the following anecdote. The Emperor Leopold the First ordered his ambassador at Rome to entreat the Pope to send him a copy of the famous *Miserere* of Allegri, which had never been performed outside the Sistine Chapel. A copy was accordingly made by the Pope's chapel-master and sent to Vienna; but its effect when performed there was so disappointing that the Emperor concluded that the Pope's chapel-master, in order to keep it a mystery, had played him false and sent some other composition. Thereupon in great wrath he sent a message to this effect to the Pope, who immediately dismissed his unfortunate chapel-master without hearing a word in his defence. After a time the poor man got one of the cardinals to plead his cause, and to explain to the Pope that the style of singing in the Sistine Chapel, and especially in performing the *Miserere,* was such as could not be expressed by notes, nor taught, nor transmitted to any other place, except by example: for which reason the piece in question must fail in its effect when performed elsewhere. The Pope, who did not understand music, could not comprehend how the same notes could sound so differently in different places; but he ordered the

Story of Notation

maestro to write down his defence, in order to send it to Vienna. The Emperor, on receiving the explanation, induced the Pope to send some of his musicians to Vienna to instruct the imperial singers in the proper way of rendering it.

We quote this story to show that the mere mechanical reading of notes is not all that is required in order to give the proper "rendering" of a composition; in this particular case something more than talent and intelligence was necessary—namely, the traditional style of performance, which the notes could not express.

Appendices.

A. AUTHORITIES REFERRED TO.

B. GLOSSARY.

C. CHRONOLOGICAL TABLE OF NOTATION.

Appendix A.

Authorities referred to.

Aaron, Peter, born at Florence in the second half of the fifteenth century, died about 1562. Canon of the Cathedral at Rimini. Published in 1525, *Trattate della natura et della cognizione di tutti gli tuoni nel canto figurato*, and in 1545 his *Lucidario in Musica*, in which he sustained a lively contest with Gafurius on the proper division of the tetrachords in the three genera—diatonic, chromatic, and enharmonic. In his *Toscanella* he gives important information on the rules of counterpoint.

Adelbold, born in the tenth century, died 1027. He was Bishop of Utrecht, and chancellor to Henry II. of Germany. He made war against the Count of Holland in order to force him to yield up possession of the island of Merwe; but being unsuccessful he returned to his diocese, built churches, cultivated science, and became one of the most learned men of his time. His treatise on music is contained in Gerbert's *Scriptores Ecclesiastici de Musica.*

Agricola, Martin, director of music in the Reformed Church at Magdeburg; born in Silesia 1486, died 1556. Author of many important works on music, from one of which, in verse, entitled, *Musica instrumentalis deudsch*, we give examples of tablature.

Alypius. A sophist of the school of Alexandria, who lived in the second century of our era. Nothing is known of his life, and his *Introduction to Music* has perished except the fifth of its seven parts, which gives the whole of the Greek

223

Story of Notation

notation, with a verbal description of each sign in order to avoid the mistakes of copyists. The MSS. of this fragment are numerous, and are found in many of the ancient libraries of Europe.

Anonymus. Many important anonymous mediæval treatises are edited by Gerbert and Coussemaker, and are referred to by numbers. The single Greek anonymous treatise on music was first edited by F. Bellermann in 1841, with copious Latin notes, and six years afterwards a French translation was published by Vincent, from MSS. in the Paris Royal Library. It is supposed to date from the first or second century of the Christian era; it gives important information as to the time-signs and rests used in Greek music, singing exercises, the modes used by various instruments, the compass of various kinds of voice, modulations, together with a good many short musical examples in the Lydian trope, of which it describes the notation.

Archytas. A Pythagorean, born at Tarentum in South Italy, a contemporary of Plato and of Dionysius, the tyrant of Syracuse. He is known to have written a work on harmonics, and another on flutes, both of which are lost. His teaching is referred to by Boethius, Ptolemy, and others.

Aristides, Quintilianus. Probably contemporary with Augustus, B.C. 63 to A.D. 14. Author of an important treatise on music in three parts, the first of which contains several examples of Greek notation.

Aristoxenus. Born at Tarentum about B.C. 354, a pupil of Aristotle, whose successor he hoped to become. He was the author of several treatises on music, of which parts of two only have survived, that on Harmonics and that on Rhythm. He asserted, in opposition to the Pythagorean school, that the tone could be divided by ear into two equal semitones, thus anticipating by more than 2000 years the modern system of tuning the organ and piano Although he gives no musical examples, his treatise on Harmonics is important in the history of notation, owing to several references to its use.

Appendix A

Bellermann, J. Friedrich, published important works on the music of ancient Greece, dealing especially with its notation, under the titles *Die Hymnen des Dionysius und Mesomedes,* 1840; *Anonymi Scriptio de Musica,* 1841 (the work referred to in Chapters I. and II.), and *Die Tonleiter und Musiknoten der Griechen,* 1847. These works placed the ancient notation in a clearer light than any previous explanations had done, and prepared the ground for the later investigations of Westphal and Gevaert.

Boethius. Born at Rome about A.D. 470, of a Consular family. He became Consul three times, and was Master of the Palace of Theodoric, who acted on his advice for many years, but becoming suspicious, threw him into prison, and put him to death. Boethius was the author of a treatise which influenced the teaching of music throughout the whole of the Middle Ages. He gives part of the Greek notation, but uses the Latin alphabet to illustrate his explanations, whence arose the expression "Boethian notation," though there never was a Boethian notation.

Caserta, Philip of, born at Caserta, near Naples, of whose life nothing is known except that he was a good singer, was the author of a treatise on notation called *De diversis figuris Notarum;* it was produced between the years 1442 and 1491, and first edited by Coussemaker.

Cerone di Bergamo, a priest, born at Bergamo in 1566, died about 1620 (?), was a singer in the Cathedral of Oristano in Sardinia, whence he went to Spain, in which country he travelled much. He was chaplain to Philip II. (husband of Mary, Queen of England) and Philip III. till 1593. In 1608 he became Chapel Master at Naples. He was the author of several works, of which *El Melopeo,* in Spanish, is the most important. Fétis, however, doubts if he was more than the editor, and says that it is in reality a translation of a work of Zarlino into Spanish.

Cleonides. Two treatises exist under the name of Euclid: one, called the "Division of the Canon," is by the famous geometrician, and is Pythagorean in its doctrines; the other an Aristoxenian treatise, now generally accepted as the work

Story of Notation

of Cleonides, of whom nothing seems to be known. Both are edited by Meibomius, under the name of Euclid; but the second has many editions under the name of Cleonides, who is often referred to as Pseudo-Euclid. Both treatises were translated into English by C. Davy, London, 1787. 2 vols.

Coussemaker, C. E. H. de, born at Bailleul 1805, died 1876, a learned musician, Member of the French Institute, Chevalier of the Legion of Honour, etc. He was the author of *Histoire de l'Harmonie au Moyen Âge*, 1852, of many other musical memoirs and pamphlets, and the editor of *Scriptorum de Musica Medii Ævi*, in 4 volumes, 1864-76, a continuation of Gerbert's *Scriptores*.

Fortlage, Charles, Doctor of Philosophy, and professor at the University of Jena, published in 1847, *Das Musikalische System der Griechen in seiner Urgestalt*, dealing with the scales of Alypius, in which he discovered the key-scale (Hypolydian), that gave the key to the deciphering of the rest, and helped to prepare the ground for Westphal, Gevaert, and others.

Franco of Cologne. Of the life of this important writer we have so little information that it is not even known which of three of the same name is the author of *Ars Cantus Mensurabilis*, though Fétis attributes it to a philosopher, mathematician, astronomer, and musician, who was born at Cologne in the eleventh century, of whose life he gives some particulars. The attribution of an *Ars Cantus Mensurabilis*, found at Milan, to Franco of Paris, is by Fétis considered as a mistake of the copyist. Riemann, however (*Gesch. der Musik. Theorie*), speaks of Franco of Paris and Franco of Cologne as two persons; and by Hieronymus de Moravia the treatise is attributed to Johannes de Burgundia. A Franco who was Prior of the Benedictine Abbey of Cologne in 1190, is perhaps the author.

Fux, John Joseph, composer and author of *Gradus ad Parnassum*, a very important work on counterpoint, was born in 1660, died 1741. He was Chapel Master to the Court of Vienna for forty years, under Leopold, Joseph I., and

Appendix A

Charles VI. His first works were for the Church, but he afterwards added instrumental music and opera to his range of composition. Charles VI. insisted on himself accompanying one of Fux's operas on the harpsichord (the place of the Capellmeister was in those days at the harpsichord), and Fux, turning over the pages for him, exclaimed, on seeing how well he played, "What a pity your Majesty is not a Capellmeister!" "It is not so bad," said Charles, "being what I am." Besides being a learned writer, Fux was a prolific composer. Fétis gives a list of his works.

Gafurius, or Gafori, or Gaforio, a learned writer on music, was born at Todi 1451, died 1522. He was the son of a soldier, and was destined for the Church; after being ordained he studied music, and after many vicissitudes of war and poverty, became a singer in the Cathedral of Milan. "His writings exercised a powerful influence on the musical studies of his day, and most of his successors quote his opinions as authoritative."—*Fétis.* He was attacked by Spataro, or Spadaro, and Aaron, on account of some of his proportions of intervals, and a long and bitterly contested strife ensued, in which many joined, and in which his side was supposed to have the victory.

Galileo, Galilei, the father of the astronomer, was a Florentine gentleman, born about 1555. He was an amateur performer on the lute and viol, had an unusual knowledge of the science and history of music, and was a friend of Bardi, in whose house originated Italian opera. In his *Discorso della Musica antica e della moderna,* 1581, he published the three Græco-Roman hymns, with Greek notation, mentioned on p. 39, from MSS. found in several libraries. These were republished with notes by Bellermann in 1841, and are described in every important history of music.

Gaudentius, "The Philosopher," an Aristoxenian, has left us a small but interesting work, entitled *Harmonic Introduction,* in which the major third is reckoned among the concords, it being a discord with the Pythagoreans, on account of its mathematical tuning. Nothing is known of the time or place of his birth; but his work was translated from

Story of Notation

Greek into Latin, as early as the fifth century of our era, by Mutianus, who also translated the Homilies of St. Chrysostom. Gaudentius probably lived some time in the third or fifth centuries A.D.

Gerbert, Abbé, born in 1720, died 1793, was a learned Benedictine of the Monastery of St. Blaise in the Black Forest. He travelled much, was in correspondence with many learned societies, was a friend of Martini the historian at Bologna, and the author of an important history of church music. In 1784 he published his *Scriptores Ecclesiastici de Musica Sacra Potissimum* in three volumes, being a collection of the ancient writers on church music, which eighty years later was continued by Coussemaker.

Gerle, Hans, a lute-maker and player of Nuremberg, published important works on Tablature between 1530 and 1552, which have now become rare. There were two lute-makers of this name contemporaries at Nuremberg, but what relation, if any, they were is not known; and there is confusion as to the dates of their death.

Gevaert, F. A., Director of the Brussels Conservatoire, is one of the most learned of living writers on ancient music. Of the three volumes of his *La Musique de l'Antiquité*, vol. i. (1875) treats exhaustively of the sources of information, the modes, tropes, nuances, and notation of the Greeks; vol. ii., 1881, is occupied with the rhythm, the instruments, and the drama of antiquity; vol. iii., 1895, deals with the transition from Greek to Christian music, analyses the early hymns and antiphons, throwing much new light on their origin.

Guido, Aretino, was born at Arezzo, not far from Rome, towards the end of the tenth century, though he has been at various times claimed as having been born in Normandy, in Germany, and at Canterbury; while Spanish historians claim that he attained his musical knowledge in Catalonia. He became a monk in the Benedictine Abbey of Pomposa near Ferrara, where he obtained a reputation for his teaching powers, which soon spread through Italy. Driven out of his abbey by the jealousy of his fellow-monks, who

228

Appendix A

poisoned the mind of the abbot against him, he made "long voyages in his exile," according to his own words. It seems doubtful where these long voyages were made: some say he went to Bremen ; in any case he ended them at Arezzo, where he retired into a Benedictine monastery. From Arezzo he unwillingly went, after having received three invitations from Pope John XIX., to Rome (see p. 87), but his health giving way, he retired to Pomposa, whose abbot now received him with friendship. It is not known when or where he died. Of his invaluable work in connection with notation we have spoken in Chapter V.

Hanboys, Hambois, Hamboys, Doctor John, eminent in music, Latin, and mathematics, is mentioned by several historians for his "notable cunning" in music. Nothing is known of his life. He wrote about 1470, *Quatuor Principalia Totius Artis*, published by Coussemaker. Burney, however, attributes this tract to Tunstede. A second work by him, in the Bodleian Library, is entitled, *Musica Magistri Franconis cum Additionibus et Opinionibus Diversorum*.

Handlo, Robert de, an English musician of whom no particulars are known, author in 1326 of *Regulæ cum Maximis Magistri Franconis, cum Additionibus aliorum Musicorum*, in dialogue form, published by Coussemaker. The ancient MS. of this work was destroyed in the fire at the Cotton Library at Westminster, but fortunately Dr. Pepusch had made a copy, which is now in the British Museum. Morley calls him Robert de Harlo.

Hermann, surnamed Contractus, on account of his being paralysed, was born in 1013 at Golgau in Suabia, and brought up at the Abbey of St. Gall. He became a Benedictine monk at Reichenau, and is said to have died about 1055. His largest work was a history of the world. As a musician he is said to be the composer of some antiphons, of the hymn, *Veni, Sancte Spiritus*, and many other proses. He is the author of a tract, entitled *Musica*, on the Greek modes, of no value, and of a work in verse, entitled *Versus Hermanni ad discernendum Cantum*, giving a key to a

Story of Notation

notation by Greek and Latin letters, used in his day to decipher the neumes. Both works are published by Gerbert.

Hothby, Hothbus, Ottobus, Hothobus, Otteby, John, an English Carmelite, produced in 1471 a work entitled, *Hothby, Anglici, Proportiones Musicæ.* It is published by Coussemaker in three parts; the third, entitled *Regulæ super Contrapunctum,* gives the rules of a mode of singing, called "visible discant," used in England.

Hucbald, Hugbald, a monk of St. Amand in Tournay, born about 840, died about 932; was either a Frenchman or Belgian by birth. He was a pupil of his uncle at St. Amand, who, in a fit of jealousy caused by his brilliant compositions, drove him from the monastery and forced him to retire to Nevers, where he opened a school of singing. After the death of his uncle he succeeded him as director of the monastic school of St. Amand. His success was great, and he was called upon to direct or found other schools; in his old age he retired to St. Amand, where he died. He is mentioned as the author of several treatises, which are published by Gerbert, but Hans Müller and Riemann (*Gesch. der Musik. Theorie,* p. 4) contest his right to *Musica enchiriadis* and *Harmonica institutio,* which have been attributed to his authorship.

Kircher, Athanasius, a learned Jesuit, was born in 1602 at Geysen, near Fulda, died 1680; author of an enormous work on music, entitled *Musurgia Universalis.* Fétis says, "This learned man shows in his writings a *bizarre* conjunction of deep knowledge in mathematics, physics, natural history, philology, and a credulous mind, greedy of the marvellous, and devoid of judgment. In his immense works the false and the true are mixed together pell-mell, but there are plenty of good and interesting things for those who take the trouble to seek them." The Thirty Years' War drove him from Germany to Avignon, and then Rome, where he spent the rest of his life in gigantic works on nearly every branch of human knowledge, and where he founded a famous museum, which is still in existence. The

Appendix A

Musurgia contains the Greek notation of the first of Pindar's Pythic odes.

Mace, Thomas, born 1619, died 1709. Little is known of his life, and the only work he appears to have published is *Musick's Monument* (see page 154, note), which treats of Psalm-singing in parish churches, and of the lute and viol, published in 1676.

Marchettus of Padua flourished at the end of the thirteenth and beginning of the fourteenth centuries. Nothing is known of his life, or of whether he was a monk or a priest. His *Brevis Compilatio in Arte Musicæ* is published in Coussemaker's third volume.

Martini, Giambattista, born at Bologna 1706, died 1784, a learned composer and theorist, and a famous teacher, was the possessor of one of the most complete musical libraries of his day, estimated by Burney at 17,000 volumes. His two most important works, frequently referred to by Burney and Hawkins, are a *History of Music*, and his work on counterpoint. A list of his compositions is given in Grove's *Dictionary*.

Meibomius, Meybaum, or Meibom, Mark, born at Tönningen 1626, died at Utrecht 1711, a learned Dutch philologist, was a professor at the University of Upsal, and librarian to Frederick III. of Denmark. He published in 1652, *Antiquæ musicæ Auctores septem*, a wonderfully correct edition of treatises by Aristoxenus, Euclid (see Cleonides), Alypius, Nicomachus, Gaudentius, Bacchius Senior, and Aristides Quintilianus, with Latin translations and copious notes. His visionary temperament led him into several unfortunate enterprises. Giving up his chair at Upsal, he endeavoured to persuade Dutch and French mariners to adopt the ancient triremes; failing in this, he came to England and endeavoured to publish a Hebrew edition of the Old Testament, corrected by himself; this also failing of success, he retired to Holland and died in poverty.

231

Story of Notation

Morley, Thomas, Mus. Bac., born about the middle of the sixteenth century, died about 1604. A pupil of Byrd, and a Gentleman of the Chapel Royal, was the author of a quaint work entitled *A Plaine and Easie Introduction to Practicall Musicke*, 1597, containing much valuable information on the old notation and the tablatures. He was the composer of many madrigals, anthems, services, lessons for the Virginals, a list of which is given in Grove's *Dictionary*.

Muris, Johannes de. According to Dr. Hugo Riemann, *Gesch. der Musik. Theorie*, im *ix.-xix. Jahrhundert*, 1898, page 235, etc., there were in the fourteenth century two musicians of this name, the Norman and the Parisian. The Norman Muris studied at Paris, but lived and taught at Oxford, whence he is also called the English De Muris. He contributed nothing new to the development of notation. The Parisian De Muris was a friend of Philip of Vitry, and the author of important works, among them *Musica Speculativa*, 1323. The works of both are published by Gerbert and Coussemaker.

Narbaez, Louis de, a Spanish musician, who published at Valladolid, in 1538, six books of tablature for the viol or vihuela, together with instructions for the use of the tablature in Spanish.

Odo, or Oddo of Clugny, a monk of noble family, who, after studying under Remi d'Auxerre, became Canon and Precentor of St. Martin de Tours in 899, and in 927 Abbot of Clugny, where he died in 942. His *Dialogus de Musica*, published by Gerbert, is an instruction book for the use of the monochord, the modes and their transpositions and formulas, to which the Latin letters, together with the Greek gamma, are arranged for the scale in the modern way, a method formerly attributed to Guido. His claim to the authorship of the *Dialogus* has, however, been contested of late in Germany—*vide* Riemann, *Gesch. der Musik. Theorie*, p. 55.

Olympus, who lived before the Trojan war, was a pupil of Marsyas, and the composer of three *nomes* or songs, which

232

Appendix A

were sung for centuries by the Greeks; and to him is attributed by Plutarch the invention of the enharmonic genus. A second Olympus was a famous flute-player of the time of Midas.

Pachymère, George, a Byzantine historian, born in 1242 at Nicæa, died about 1310. He was a priest of the Greek Church, and the author of a work on music in fifty-two chapters, published by Vincent in his *Notices et Extraits des Manuscrits du Bibliothèque du Roi,* 1847.

Plutarch, the Greek historian, born at Chæronæa in Bœotia about A.D. 49, was the author of a treatise on music, published with a German translation and notes by Westphal in 1865, and with an anonymous English translation in 1822, at Chiswick, by C. Whittingham. It is in the form of a dialogue treating of the history of Greek music, which, together with the work of Athenæus, gives the most important information extant on the subject. Plutarch is also the author of another musical work, which treats of the Pythagorean musical numbers described in Plato's *Timæus.*

Pollux, Julius, a Greek grammarian and rhetorician, born at Naucratis in Egypt in the second century after Christ, died at Athens in the early part of the third century, was the author of a work in six volumes called *Onomasticon,* in the form of a lexicon; edited by Bekker at Berlin, 1846. The second and fourth books contain several chapters on music.

Polymnastus, of Colophon in Ionia, was a follower of Terpander, and composed flute airs, pro-odes, elegiacs, and elegies. Plutarch counts him amongst the founders of the second Spartan school of music, in which the enharmonic genus had a place.

Prosdoscimus de Beldemandis was in 1422 a professor of Philosophy of Padua, his native town. He is the author of several treatises on *musica mensurata* and counterpoint, published by Coussemaker. Fétis considers that his works owe their chief importance to the fact that their author, being contemporary with Dufay and Binchois, belonged to

Story of Notation

one of the most important epochs in musical history. The dates of his birth and death and particulars seem to be unknown.

Ptolemy, Claudius, the celebrated Greek astronomer, the events of whose life are unknown, except that his last recorded astronomical observation can be traced to the 22nd of March A.D. 141. He was the author of a treatise on music in three parts, of which MSS. are found in most great European libraries; the work was published with a Latin translation and notes in 1680, by Wallis, an Oxford mathematician, together with a mass of mathematical (Pythagorean) calculations of intervals. This work gives a clear exposition of the transposition of the trope, our descending minor scale, to all the keys possible to the modern keyboard, together with other details of Greek music not mentioned elsewhere.

Pythagoras was born at Samos about B.C. 580. He studied philosophy in Phœnicia and Egypt, returned to Greece, where he studied at Sparta; finally went to Italy and established a cult of philosophy at Crotona, where he had many disciples. Persecution of the new sect arose; the Pythagoreans were slain or driven into exile, and the founder was martyred at Metapontus. Pythagoras, like Socrates, wrote nothing; and his musical doctrines appear to have suffered modification at the hands of ancient writers. He taught that numbers were the soul of the universe; that the planets in their courses made a "celestial concert" of consonances analogous to the musical intervals of the octave, fifth, fourth, etc.; and that, therefore, the musical scale must be regulated by mathematical proportions. This resulted in the impossibility of modulation, while it made the major third (called by the Pythagoreans a *ditone*) one of the harshest of discords. The Aristoxenian school was probably the result of the protests of practical musicians against such a cramping doctrine. Aristides Quintilianus attributes a certain form of notation to Pythagoras; it is possible that the Pythagoreans used it for their own purposes.

234

Appendix A

Strozzio or **Strozzi,** Gregory, an abbé, doctor of canon law, and apostolic protonotary; born at Naples, where he was living in the second half of the seventeenth century. In 1683 he published *Elementorum Musicæ Praxis,* in which he treats of the music of his day, and gives a number of strange proportions for time (see page 183), perhaps the result of his not being a practical musician. He also published a book of organ and harpsichord music, of good quality, in 1687.

Terpander, called the Lesbian. It is not known when he lived, but all ancient writers are agreed as to his merits as a musician. He gained many prizes for music in the games, and is said to have calmed a sedition at Sparta by the charm of his songs with the kithara. His compositions, called *nomes,* were very famous throughout Greece, and were used as opening pieces for the public games. He is said to have introduced the heptachord scale for the lyre (see page 9), and some writers assert that he wrote in notation the lyric intonations for the whole of the Homeric poems.

Tinctor, John, the date of whose birth is variously given, died at Naples in 1476; was a native of Flanders. Besides being a learned writer, he was one of the first professors, if not the founder, of the public music school at Naples, said to be the first of its kind in Italy. Amongst his works are the earliest known musical dictionary, *Terminorum Musicæ diffinitorium,* published with a German translation by Bellermann in the *Jahrbücher der Mus. Wissenschaft,* vol. i., and by Coussemaker; and a *Proportionale Musices* in three books, treating of the proportions of notes in the notation of his time.

Vincent, A. J. H., born in 1797, a member of the French Academy, and Librarian to the Ministry of Public Instruction, was the author of many pamphlets and writings on the music of the ancients and of the early Church, and the publisher of several ancient MSS. He sustained a lengthy controversy with Fétis on the question of whether the ancients made use of harmonic combinations of sounds;

Story of Notation

the question was practically settled by Westphal, whose opinion is now generally accepted, that the ancients used no harmony of voices (except that of the octave), but that the lyre occasionally sounded single notes above the voice, which were not in octaves with it.

Virdung, a Bavarian priest and organist, who lived at Basle during the first decades of the sixteenth century. He was the author of *Musica Getutscht und Ausgezogen* in quaint Bavarian dialect, intended as the preliminary to a much larger work, which, however, was never written. It describes the instruments in use, and gives examples of tablatures for them (see pages 150, 179).

Vitry, Philip of, lived between 1290 and 1361, was Bishop of Meaux, and a famous composer of motets, lays, and rondos; author of a treatise on the *Ars Nova* of his day, called *Liber Musicalium*, though Riemann considers that the *Ars Nova*, in which the rules for counterpoint became more strict, was in use before his time (*Geschichte der Musik. Theorie*, chap. ii.). Burney (*History*, vol. ii. p. 209) shows that several ancient writers attributed to him the invention of the minim.

Westphal, Rudolph, a professor at the University of Moscow (died about 1889), was amongst the most learned of modern investigators of ancient music, especially with regard to its rhythm. He showed that the principles of rhythmical construction of phrases, and even of complete works of art, are essentially the same in the dramas of the ancients and the compositions of modern classical musicians, from Sebastian Bach onwards. He was also a strong advocate of the view that the Aristoxenians made use of equal temperament, in which he is followed by Gevaert, Riemann, and most modern authorities on ancient music.

Zarlino, Joseph, born in 1519 at Chioggia (though Burney says he was born in 1540), died 1599, was organist of St. Mark's at Venice, and one of the most famous theorists of his day. " Il quale nella teoria e nella composizione è senza pari "

Appendix A

(Sansovino); "Famoso restauratore della musica in tutta Italia" (Foscarini). In connection with the history of notation, his *Istituzioni Harmoniche*, in 448 folio pages, published at Venice in 1558, gives much information, both with regard to his own and previous times. It was followed by several other works on theory, especially with regard to the proportions of intervals, on which he was attacked by his pupil Galileo. He was also the author of philosophical and theological treatises.

Appendix B.

Glossary.

Alto Clef, the name given to the C clef when it is placed on the middle line of the stave.

Arsis, the weak portion of a bar or measure.

B, German for B flat, from the mediæval *b rotundum*, as opposed to *b quadrum*, which in Germany is called h or H.

Bar. The perpendicular lines across the stave to mark the measures began to come into use at the beginning of the seventeenth century in the staff notation; but they had been used for more than a century previously in the tablatures. Morley, who died in 1604, is probably one of the first to use the word "bar" in its modern sense of "measure."

Baritone Clef, the name given to the F clef when it is placed on the middle line of the stave.

Bass, the vocal part called *bassus* lying below the Plainsong, or Tenor, was of later invention than the Discant and Treble.

Bass Clef, the name given to the F clef when, as in all modern music, it is placed on the fourth line of the stave.

Bémol, the French for flat, as *si bémol*, etc.

B quadrum, Latin for B natural.

Brevis, our Breve, a note of double, and in mediæval music three times, the value of the Semibreve; it is now almost obsolete.

B rotundum, Latin for B flat.

238

Appendix B

Cantus figuralis, the "figurated" counterpoint that accompanied the melody of the Plainsong.

Cantus firmus, Fixed song, Plainsong, the Gregorian melody on which early contrapuntal music was based.

Cantus planus, Plainsong, generally known as Gregorian music.

Chromatic, "coloured," a Greek form of scale in which certain degrees were altered in pitch. The word is used in modern music for a series of semitones, or for harmonies in which many accidentals occur.

Clavichord, "keyed string," an instrument derived from the monochord, in which keys, instead of a plectrum, caused strings to sound. Since its strings were struck, it must not be confused with the harpsichord, of later invention, in which the strings were plucked.

Clef, the "Key" letter placed at the beginning of every stave to unlock the secrets of its notes, according to old writers.

Conjunct System, a series of seven scale degrees, containing two similar tetrachords having a sound in common, thus—

$$\overbrace{E\ F\ G\ A}$$
$$B\ C\ D\ \underbrace{E}$$

Crocheta, the Crotchet, of one-third or one-half the value of the Minima; it seems to have been invented by the Englishman Hamboys, about A.D. 1470. Purists objected that a note smaller than the smallest (*minima*) could not exist.

Diatonic, a scale proceeding chiefly by tones.

Diaphony, Discord, *i.e.* all intervals except the octave, fifth, and fourth. Owing to the peculiarity of Pythagorean tuning, the major and minor thirds and sixths were reckoned among the diaphonies.

Diése, the French for sharp, as *C diése,* etc.

Diesis, an interval smaller than a semitone.

Direct, a sign formerly used at the end of a stave to indicate the position of the first note on the stave next below.

Dis, properly speaking, the German for D sharp; but under the influence of the tablatures, in which each sound had only a single sign, Dis was used for E flat. In 1805 Beethoven's

Story of Notation

Eroica symphony was announced on the programmes of two concerts at Vienna as "Sinfonie in Dis."

Discantus, the part added above the Plainsong in the early days of Counterpoint. The soprano part is still called Diskant in Germany.

Disjunct System. A series of eight scale degrees, having no sound in common, and embracing two similar tetrachords; our major scale furnishes an example of a disjunct system—

$$\overbrace{C\ D\ E\ F,}\ \overbrace{G\ A\ B\ C}$$

Dorian Octave, the sounds given by the white keys of the pianoforte from E to *e*. Boethius, however, and after him all the Church musicians, applied the name Dorian to the scale from D to *d*.

Double Bar, the ancient rest placed at the end of a composition, or the end of an important section.

Dragma, a lozenge-shaped note with tails at each angle, sometimes used for a semibreve in mediæval times.

Driven Notes, a term used by Playford and others for syncopation.

Enharmonic, a Greek form of tetrachord, in which the semitone was divided into quarter-tones.

Expression Words were used in the tenth century by Romanus and others. They then entirely disappeared until the seventeenth century, since which period they have been constantly increasing in number.

False Music, Feigned Music, Musica Ficta, Musica Inusitata, music in which certain intervals were raised or lowered by a semitone to suit the harmonic combinations. As these alterations produced sounds that were not given by the monochord, they were at first not written. False music embraces all flats except B flat, and all sharps.

Fermata, see Pause.

Fixed Sounds, in the Greek scale, those sounds which remained fixed in all the three genera—that is to say, the highest and lowest sounds of tetrachords, together with Proslambanomenos.

Flat, the sign which shows that a note is to be lowered by a

Appendix B

semitone. In Latin it is *mollis*, soft; in French, *bémol*; in German, *be*; showing in the two latter languages its connection with the note B flat, the only flat admitted in the early centuries of the Church.

Free Rhythm, an ancient form of music, in which Latin prose was sung without being influenced by the measure of music A modern example is found in the "Reciting Note" of the Anglican Chant.

French Violin Clef, the name given to the G clef when it is placed on the middle line of the stave.

Fusa, a name used in tablatures for the semiquaver.

Guidonian Hand, a figure of the left hand, on which were placed the names of the scale degrees according to their hexachordal arrangement, and pointed to by the teacher of singing. The principle has been revived in the "Modulator" of the Tonic Sol-faists, the degrees of which are named by Guidonian syllables, and pointed out by the teacher.

Gymel, twin song, an early form of part-singing in thirds and sixths, apparently only used in England.

H, German for B natural, since the old form of square *b* was something like *h*.

Harmony, in Greek meant a scale, such as the Dorian, Phrygian, etc.

Heptachord, a scale succession of seven notes. Our descending minor scale consists of the Heptachord of Terpander, completed by the addition of a note below it; and this Heptachord contains two tetrachords. See Tetrachord.

Hexachord, which must not be confounded with the Heptachord, consists of the first six sounds of the major scale, which were used in certain combinations by Guido of Arezzo to teach sight-singing. See page 79.

Hoket, Hoquet, Hocketus, an ancient form of composition, in which the course of the melody was interrupted by frequent rests.

Hypate, the "highest"—*i.e.*, longest string of the Greek tetrachord, and therefore the lowest sound.

Story of Notation

Imperfect Mood, Time, Prolation, the division of the longer notes into two of the next in value—*i.e.*, Duple measure.

Kithara, an elaborate form of the lyre.
Krouma, the accompaniment to a song, played by the lyre.

Larga, a note containing nine longas, apparently invented by John Hamboys. It does not appear to have been much used.
Legato. The slur, or legato sign took the place of the old ligatures early in the eighteenth century.
Lichanos, the third string of the tetrachord, plucked with the forefinger.
Ligature, a sign indicating that two or more scale degrees were to be sung to the same syllable. It has been replaced in modern notation by the " Bind " or " Slur," called in Italian *Legato*, from *Ligatura*.
Locrian or Common Octave, represented by the notes A to *a* of the pianoforte.
Longa, a note of three times (or double) the value of the Breve.
Lydian Octave is represented by the modern C major scale. Boethius is responsible for miscalling the octave F to *f* the Lydian mode.

Maxima, a note of the value of three or two "longs."
Measured Music, music measured according to the laws of metre and rhythm, as opposed to Gregorian music or Plainsong, in which the notes showed no measure. Of late years attempts have been made to give time-values to pure Gregorian notation, the varying forms of which are derived from the neumes, and not from measured music.
Mese, the " middle " sound of the Greek musical system, the A to which we tune the violoncello. Mese was also used in the sense of the Gregorian Dominant, the note most used in melody, according to Aristotle. Some writers have seen in it a "keynote" in the modern sense; but the keynote should be more properly sought in Hypate.
Mezzo-soprano Clef, the name given to the C clef when it is placed on the second line of the stave.

242

Appendix B

Minima, our Minim, a note of one-third or of half the value of the Semibreve. It came into use in the thirteenth century, being mentioned by Walter Odington about 1275.

Mixolydian Octave, the notes B to *b*. Boethius and the Church musicians, however, call G to *g* the Mixolydian mode.

Monochord, an instrument in which a string was stretched over a scale of alphabetical letters. By placing a movable bridge, or a rod, under the string at the points indicated by the letters, the required sound could be produced. The monochord was for centuries used in teaching Plainsong and sight-singing.

Mood, or Mode, time measurement of which the longa formed the basis. Mode is also used for Octave-system and Trope, as the Dorian mode.

Motet, a form of composition whose modern English representative is the Cathedral anthem.

Movable Sounds, in the Greek scale those sounds which were altered to suit the different genera, as our "third" is altered to suit the major or minor mode. The second and third sounds of each tetrachord were movable (and are still in the Greek church), the first and fourth being fixed.

Natural, the sign which originally stood for B natural, *i.e.* a square-shaped *b*; afterwards used to restore a note that has been affected by a sharp or flat. The hexachord beginning on C was called *naturale*, hence our C major key is called the "natural key." The natural is called in German *quadrat*, in French *becarré* (*b* squared). Duple Rhythm began to be called "Natural Time" in the beginning of the sixteenth century.

Nete, the highest sound of tetrachords lying above Mese.

Neume, or Neuma, a sign, equivalent to the Latin *Nota*.

Notation, the art of representing musical sounds in writing, from *Nota*, a sign.

Note properly signifies a written sign, indicating a sound; but it is used of the sound itself, and hence of the key of an instrument, which produces the sound.

Organisers, priests who travelled from church to church to sing the organum.

243

Story of Notation

Organum, the earliest form of part-singing, in which the melody was sung by two or more voices at the interval of a fourth or fifth, as well as an octave.

Parhypate, "next to the highest," the lowest sound but one of the Greek tetrachord. See Hypate.

Pause. In Latin, German, Italian, this word means a Rest. In English it is used for the sign called in Italian *Fermata*, indicating that a note is to be held beyond its normal value. The Fermata sign is used by Playford on a full close, and is thus found in some music of the eighteenth century.

Perfect Mood, Time, Prolation, time measurement by the division of the longer notes into three of the next in value, *i.e.* Triple measure.

Phonetic Notation, any notation in which sounds are represented by alphabetical letters, figures, or words.

Pricksong, an English expression for measured music, which was "pricked" on the parchment by its composer.

Proportion, an old term for time signature, referring to the arithmetical fractions placed at the beginning of the stave. Thus, the fraction ¾ means that the measure or bar is to the semibreve in the proportion of three to four ; or, in other words, the value of the bar is three-quarters that of the semibreve.

Phrygian Octave, the octave from D to *d* of the pianoforte without black keys ; but Boethius and his successors applied the term "Phrygian mode" to the octave E to *e*.

Pictorial Notation, any notation in which the rise and fall of melody is depicted by the higher or lower position of written signs, and time-value is represented by varying the shapes of the signs.

Plainsong, a name for Gregorian music.

Plectrum, an instrument used by the ancients to pluck the strings of the lyre, etc. In the harpsichord it is called a "Jack," and consists of a wooden upright to which a quill is attached, which acts on the string in the same way as the ancient plectrum.

Plica, a kind of ligature used with the "liquid" letters of the alphabet, the sound of which was carried into that of the

Appendix B

succeeding syllable, as is sometimes heard in uneducated singing of the present day.

Pneuma, a breathing, a breath; used of passages in Plainsong which are sung with the breath only, and without words.

Point. This word is used in many senses, *e.g.* for notes, which were anciently called Points; Point of Division, which altered the relative position of long and short notes; Point of Perfection, which lengthened a note of two-time value to three-time; Point of Addition, which had the same effect; and Point of Demonstration, which is obscure, but seems to be a means of showing *ritardando.*

Prolation, time measurement of which the breve formed the basis.

Proprietas, or Propriety, the chief note of a ligature, which was long or short, according to its position with regard to the other notes, called Improprieties.

Psalm, a song accompanied by the lyre, when the latter was played with the finger-tips instead of a plectrum.

Psaltery, a mediæval stringed instrument of the nature of the dulcimer. The name arises from the Psalterion, a kind of lyre played with the fingers. See Psalm.

Proslambanomenos, the note "added" below the Heptachord of Terpander to complete the Octochord or Diapason. The Octochord thus formed became the "Common" scale of the Greek musical system, and was adopted as the basis of the Church system. When Latin alphabetical letters took the place of the old Greek names of sounds, Proslambanomenos was called A, the Heptachord being named B, C, D, E, F, G, *a*; and the keyboards of organs, clavichords, etc., which were originally labelled with the letters, have retained this alphabetical nomenclature to the present day. The keyboards of early mediæval organs commenced at B, Proslambanomenos, or A, being deemed a superfluous sound, and outside the range of tetrachords.

Pycnon, "compressed," the three lowest sounds of the tetrachord, whose intervals varied with the different genera.

Quadruplum, a fourth part, added above the Triplum, or Treble.

Story of Notation

Quaver was called in the old tablatures a semiminim, and figured by an upright stroke with two crooks.

Repetition Dots first appeared in the tablatures, whence they were imported into the staff notation.

Rest. The rests have scarcely varied their shape from the earliest times, but they are larger now than formerly. The modern "Double Bar" was originally a rest, showing the conclusion of a piece or a section.

Semiminim, a name used in tablatures for the quaver.

Score. Vertical lines were "scored" at various intervals through the great staves of twelve to twenty lines in the Middle Ages, to guide the eye; and in more modern times, when a large number of vocal or instrumental parts began to be written on the same page, the bar-lines were "scored" through all the staves for the same purpose, the music thus written being called a "Score."

Sharp, the sign which shows that a note is to be raised by a semitone. In Latin it is called *Crux*, a cross; in German, *Kreuz;* in French, *Dièse*, from Diesis. It was originally a modification of the square *b*, and gradually arrived at the shape familiar to us.

Signature, signs placed at the beginning of the stave to indicate the rhythmical form, and the key. Time signatures appeared at a very early period in the form of circles, semicircles, etc., which in the sixteenth and seventeenth centuries gave way to numerals, the "broken circle" being however retained for Duple rhythm. Key signatures began to appear in the sixteenth century, and were for a time somewhat ambiguous in their meaning.

Soprano Clef, the name given to the C clef when it is placed on the lowest line of the stave.

Species of Octave or Tetrachord refers to the distribution of tones and semitones therein. In ecclesiastical music the species of octave is called the mode.

Staccato Signs first appeared in the works of J. S. Bach, Couperin, and Rameau.

Appendix B

Staff or Stave, the series of horizontal lines on which musical notes are written. At the present day the stave of five lines is universal in all music except Gregorian; but for some centuries any number of lines from one to twenty-four were used, the writer frequently adding a new line when the melody overstepped those he had already drawn.

Suspirium, "an apparent rest," according to Hieronymus de Moravia; in reality, a breathing place.

Symphony, a concord, *i.e.* the intervals of the octave, fifth, and fourth. In modern music the word Symphony is applied to the most important form of orchestral music.

Tablature, a form of instrumental notation used in the sixteenth and seventeenth centuries. See Chapter IX.

Tenor, the holding part, Plainsong or Gregorian melody, when used as a basis for contrapuntal compositions.

Tenor Clef, the name given to the C clef when it is placed on the fourth line of the stave.

Tetrachord, a scale or succession of four sounds embracing two tones and a semitone. Our major scale consists of two tetrachords superposed; our minor descending scale also consists of two tetrachords, having a note in common and a note "added" below the lower tetrachord. See Proslambanomenos, Heptachord.

Thesis, the down beat, or strong portion of a measure.

Time or Tempus, time measurement of which the semibreve formed the basis.

Triplum, Treble, the third part, sung above the Discantus, which was above the Plainsong or Tenor.

Trite, the third string of the tetrachord, counting downwards; only applied to tetrachords lying above Mese.

Trope, the series of sounds of two octaves from A to *a'*, including *b* flat. The trope could be transposed to any pitch, and practically corresponded to our "Key."

Appendix C.

Chronological Table of Notation.

About B.C. 671	Terpander adds a second tetrachord to the one already existing on the lyre, thus producing a heptachord; and each string has a special name.
Between B.C. 671 and 600	The heptachord is extended by the addition of tetrachords, to a compass of two octaves, called the Greater Perfect System, and to a compass of eleven sounds, called the Lesser Perfect System.[1] The instrumental notation invented (probably by Polymnastus of Colophon),[2] by adapting part of the old Attic alphabet to the musical scale.
B.C. 408	Composition of the drama " Orestes," by Euripides, of whose music a few bars have been accidentally preserved, from a copy made in the time of Augustus.
B.C. 403	The neo-Ionic alphabet becomes legally established for official use at Athens; and probably about the same time its letters are applied to the musical scale as a vocal notation, the old Attic letters being retained for instruments.[3]

[1] Gevaert, *La Musique de l'Antiquité*, vol. i. p. 125.
[2] R. Westphal, *Die Mus. des Gr. Alterthums*, p. 117.
[3] Westphal, *loc. cit.*, p. 174.

Appendix C

About B.C. 300	The earliest existing treatise on Music written by Aristoxenus of Tarentum, in which the use of tables of notation, called catapycnosis, is condemned, because students are apt to think that the learning of the notation is the whole art of music.[1]
About B.C. 120	Composition of a " Hymn to Apollo," of which the notation and words have been discovered, engraved on stone, in the Treasury of the Athenians at Delphi. Of this important composition about ninety bars in $\frac{5}{8}$ time are sufficiently well preserved to be capable of performance with only a few unimportant restorations.
About A.D. 100	A short hymn of this period has recently been discovered at Tralles, near Ephesus, engraved on a marble pillar, set up by one Seikilos. It contains vocal notation with time and accent signs.
About A.D. 117 to 138	Three hymns, to Calliope, Helios, and Nemesis, the first of which is attributed to Dionysius, the others to Mesomedes, two poets who lived under Hadrian. The MSS. with vocal notation, which are found in several European libraries, are in sufficiently good preservation for performance.
About A.D. 200	Alypius writes an " Introduction to Music," of which a portion is preserved, containing tables of the notation of the fifteen tropes in the three genera, forty-five tables in all. As he not only gives the forms of each instrumental and vocal sign, but also describes them in words, his work is the most trustworthy and complete authority in existence on the ancient notation.

[1] Aristoxenus, *Stoicheia* (Meibom.), pp. 38, etc.

Story of Notation

At unknown dates, during the first few centuries of the Christian era.	Bacchius Senior writes a catechism of music, using notation, both vocal and instrumental, to explain the intervals. Aristides Quintilianus, in a long treatise on music, gives several examples of the notation of Alypius, and another notation which he ascribes to the Pythagoreans. An unknown writer, usually referred to as "Anonymus," quotes many examples of vocal exercises in notation, and gives signs for rests, accents, long and short notes, staccato, legato, etc. This treatise is therefore very important. Gaudentius, a philosopher, writes an "Introduction," at the end of which he gives the notation of the Hypolydian, Hyperlydian, Æolian, and Hypoæolian tropes, in the Diatonic Genus only, agreeing with the tables of Alypius.
About A.D. 510	Boethius, a philosopher and Roman Consul, writes a treatise on music, in which he quotes some of the Greek notation, but shows that it had gone out of use in his day. As nothing had yet been invented to take its place, he uses Latin letters for reference, but in no regular order; hence a "Boethian notation" has been wrongly attributed to him.
About A.D. 555	The Neumatic notation, in which Greek accents were used to show the rise and fall of the voice pictorially, appears to have begun about this time, under Byzantine influence.
About A.D. 850	The Antiphonary of St. Gall was written, with complete Neumatic notation and expression signs.

Appendix C

A.D. 900 to 1000	Attempts were made by Hucbald, Odo of Tomières, Hermann Contractus, and many others, to invent a more satisfactory notation than that of the neumes, by means of alphabetical letters.
About A.D. 990	Birth of Guido of Arezzo.
A. D. 1000 to 1100	The Montpellier Antiphonary was provided with alphabetical letters from *a* to *k* above the neumes. A manuscript, now in the Bodleian Library, was provided with alphabetical letters, *a* to *k* above the words, and without neumes.
	A local system of seven lines, representing the seven sounds of Terpander's heptachord, and bearing dots for notes, seems to have been used about this time in Sicily. It, however, led to nothing.
	In the first decades of this century, Guido of Arezzo adopted the naming of sounds by the first seven letters of the Latin alphabet, which system has continued to the present day. As Proslambanomenos was the lowest sound of the Greek system, he called it A, but a still lower sound, he called by the Greek letter Gamma. Hence the word Gamut for scale.
	He also drew parallel lines through the neumes, which lines became the staff of modern music; and on each line he wrote a letter, called a clavis or clef. For teaching singing he used the well-known syllables, *Ut, Re, Mi, Fa, Sol, La*, arranging them in hexachords, according to that order of sounds which was afterwards known as the major scale. The first half of the eleventh century, therefore, may be said to have seen the birth of modern notation as regards its representation of intervals.

251

Story of Notation

A. D. 1100 to 1200	Owing to the development of Organum into Discant, the necessity arose for measuring the relative length of sounds, as well as deciding their intervals. The Punctum of the neumes became both a square note, called a breve, and a lozenge, called a semibreve; the virga was given a square head, and became a "long," equal to two breves.
A. D. 1200 to 1300	A notation for Triple Measure was invented by making the long contain three breves, and the breve three semibreves; and the new valuation was called Perfect Measure, the older duple valuation being called Imperfect. Rests were invented. False music began to be used.
About 1250	"Sumer is icumen in," composed by John of Reading. The date of "Ars Cantus Mensurabilis," by Franco of Cologne, is unknown; it was perhaps between 1230 and 1250.
1274	Marchettus of Padua describes red notes as showing change of mood, or alteration of the normal value of the notes. The sharp, as well as chromatic passages are used by the same author.
About 1275	The minim invented by Walter Odington, monk of Evesham.
A.D. 1300 to 1400	A great number of treatises on Measured Music are written, of which Coussemaker prints forty.

252

Appendix C

A.D. 1321	Johannes de Muris, the Norman, uses alphabetical letters instead of notes, on a four-lined stave. The "figure" of the semibreve much confused at this period. The circle, or three upright lines, to show triple measure, and the half-circle, or two upright lines, to show duple measure, seem to have come into use shortly before this date. At the same time musicians were not unanimous, some using letters, others circles enclosing lines, etc.
1322	An effort to suppress semibreves and minims by a Papal Bull.
1326	Robert de Handlo endeavours to indicate false music by varying the position of the stems of notes.
About 1413	The "Direct" used at the end of each stave to show the first note of the following stave, by Prosdoscimus de Beledmandis.
About 1460	Conrad Paulmann invents the tablature for the lute described by Virdung in 1511.
1470	The crotchet described, and perhaps invented, by John Hamboys.
About 1475	John Hothby reduces the "points" or dots from four to two in number.
1512	Arnold Schlick publishes the first printed organ tablature book.
1529	Sebald Heyden, of Nuremberg, proposes to abolish the clefs.

253

Story of Notation

254

Appendix C

About A.D. 1700	The square and lozenge notation was rapidly giving way to the oval and round-headed notes of the present day.
1720-30	Appearance of the staccato sign in the works of Couperin, J. S. Bach, and others.
1730	The nineteenth edition of Playford's "Introduction" refers to the running together of the crooks of a succession of quavers (in the modern method) as "the new tyed note."
1735	Mattheson proposes the modern form of the double sharp.
1743	J. J. Rousseau endeavours to carry out Souhaitty's proposal to abolish notes.
1758	Adlung says that the circle with a dot, indicating triple measure, is rapidly disappearing.
1769	Jacob, a Frenchman, proposes to abolish the clefs, and to use figures for notes.
1774	The treatise on Counterpoint, of Martini, published, with the old square notation, and ligatures; probably their last use, except in plainsong.
1775	C. P. E. Bach gives a doubled G clef in the flute part in his oratorio *Die Israeliten in der Wüste*, to show that two flutes are to play from the same stave.
1776	The Abbé de Cassagne proposes to abolish all clefs except G.

Story of Notation

<table>
<tr><td>About A.D. 1790</td><td>The soprano clef began to be given up in favour of the G clef, for the treble part of English anthems.</td></tr>
<tr><td>1792</td><td>Rohleder, a German, endeavours to abolish the names of notes for piano music by giving black notes to black keys, and white notes to white keys; a new keyboard being invented to suit the notation.</td></tr>
<tr><td>1818</td><td>Galin, of Bordeaux, invents a method of teaching the notation by numerals, the system now used in the elementary schools of France.</td></tr>
<tr><td>1845</td><td>Miss Sarah Glover publishes her invention of the Tonic Sol-fa notation.</td></tr>
</table>

Index.

Index

Delphic Hymn to Apollo, 27 *and note,* 39

Demotz, Abbé, proposes to suppress the staff, 202

Diaphony, the ancient term for discord, 18 *note,* 65

Diastematic or pictorial notation, 11

Diatonic, 3; of Polymnastus, 21; middle soft, 22

Dièse, 117

Diesis, 22; notation of, 23; a mediæval term for the sharp, 117

Direct, 133, 139

Discantus, discant, 91, 94, 107, 109; extempore, 146; term for soprano voice-part, 139; applied to viol, 158; to flute, 159

Disjunct system, 9

Distropha, 60

Division of mood, 97; is the origin of the bar-line, 98

Dorian alphabet used for notation, 15

Dorian tetrachord, 8; harmony, 26, 29; trope, 35

Dot after a note, 133; of perfection, 149; of repetition, 151; peculiar use of, 174

Dots or points used to indicate fingering, 157, 161

Double bar, 176

Double flat, 144

Double long, 96

Double sharp, 143

Double-tailed notes, 133

Dragma, 124, *and note*

Driven notes, 175

Dufay uses open notes to save time, 181

Dutch Reformed Church, 181

E FLAT, mollis, 115, 140

Early English Harmony, 165, 167

Early line notation, 69

Eastern Church, and scale of twelve semitones, 139; music of, 192

Egyptians, 1

Eitner's rules for false music, 141

Enharmonic genus, 3, 22; falls out of use, 39; notation of, 23-25

Epigoneion, 8, 16

Epiphonus, 60; becomes the plica, 101

Equal temperament, 20, *and note;* known to the Greeks, 36

Expression signs, 53, 187, 189; in tablatures, 158

Extempore discant, 147

F NOTATION, 62, 67

False music, feigned music. *See* Musica falsa

Fauxbourdon, Faburden, 91

Fermata, 177

Fétis's criticism of Galin's notation, 206

Figures, an ancient term for notes, 95

Figured bass, 183

Fixed sounds, 20, 23, 32

Flat used to contradict a sharp, 117

Florid chant, 46

Flute prohibited in early church, 43

Foot, in poetry, 138

Franco of Cologne, 91-106, 114, 119

Free rhythm, 53, 106

French and Italian notation, disagreements between, 131, 134

French names of notes, 177

Fusa, in tablature, 149

Fux, Gradus ad Parnassum, 181

Story of Notation

Index

Index

Story of Notation

Index

THE END.